MW01041712

EDMONTON & NORTHERN ALBERTA

ANDREW HEMPSTEAD

Contents

EDMONTON &
NORTHERN ALBERTA

EDMONTON

Edmonton, Alberta's capital, sits in the center of the province, surrounded by the vast natural resources that have made the city unabashedly wealthy. It's a vibrant cultural center and a gateway to the north, but its reputation as a boomtown may be its defining characteristic. Boomtowns are a phenomenon unique to the West—cities that have risen from the surrounding wilderness, oblivious to hardship, pushed forward by dreams of the incredible wealth to be made overnight by pulling riches from the earth. Most boomtowns disappear as quickly as they rise, but not Edmonton. The proud city saw not one but three major booms in the 20th century and has grown into one of the world's largest northerly cities. Its population has mushroomed to over 740,000 (one million if the surrounding area is included),

making it the sixth-largest city in Canada. Although Calgary is the administrative and business center of the province's billion-dollar petroleum industry, Edmonton is the technological, service, and supply center.

The North Saskatchewan River Valley winding through the city has been largely preserved as a 27-kilometer (17-mile) greenbelt—the largest urban park system in Canada. Rather than the hodgepodge of slums and streets you might expect in a boomtown, the modern city of Edmonton has been extremely well designed and well built, with an eye toward the future. The downtown area sits on a spectacular bluff overlooking the river-valley park system. Silhouetted against the deep-blue sky, a cluster of modern glass-and-steel highrises makes a dynamic contrast to the historic

© ANDREW HEMPSTEAD

HIGHLIGHTS

◖ **Muttart Conservatory:** Four glass pyramids make up this interesting attraction across from downtown. It's especially fun to visit in winter, to feel the humidity of the jungle pyramid while snow covers the outside grounds (page 19).

◖ **Fort Edmonton Park:** Immerse yourself in the past at this sprawling riverside attraction, where costumed interpreters add to the historical atmosphere (page 21).

◖ **Old Strathcona:** Edmonton's best-preserved historic district centers on Whyte Avenue, a continuous strip of trendy boutiques, funky cafés, and interesting bookstores (page 22).

◖ **Royal Alberta Museum:** Exhibits in one of Canada's premier museums cover Alberta's one billion years of natural and human history (page 22).

◖ **West Edmonton Mall:** Simply put, there is no place like it in Canada – the world's largest shopping and indoor amusement complex truly does have something for everyone (page 25).

◖ **River Valley Park System:** Escape from the mall and other indoor attractions by spending time within a system of interconnecting parks along the North Saskatchewan River (page 29).

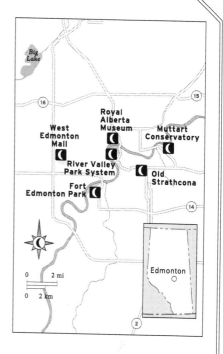

LOOK FOR ◖ TO FIND RECOMMENDED SIGHTS, ACTIVITIES, DINING, AND LODGING.

granite Alberta Legislature Building and the lush valley floor below.

Edmonton is home to the University of Alberta, and it's hosted events such as the 1978 Commonwealth Games, 1983 World University Games, 1996 World Figure Skating Championships, and the 2001 World Championships in Athletics. So it comes as no surprise that Edmonton has some of Canada's best cultural facilities. Each week during summer, a festival of some sort takes place within the city. But the city's biggest attraction is the ultimate shopping experience of West

Edmonton Mall, the world's largest shopping and amusement complex.

ORIENTATION

Highway 2 from Calgary enters Edmonton from the south and divides just north of Gateway Park Tourist Information Centre. At that point, it becomes known as **Gateway Boulevard** (also called **103rd Street**). Southbound, it's **Calgary Trail (104th Street).** From the south, you can get to West Edmonton Mall and Highway 16 West, without going through downtown, by taking **Anthony Henday Drive,**

EDMONTON

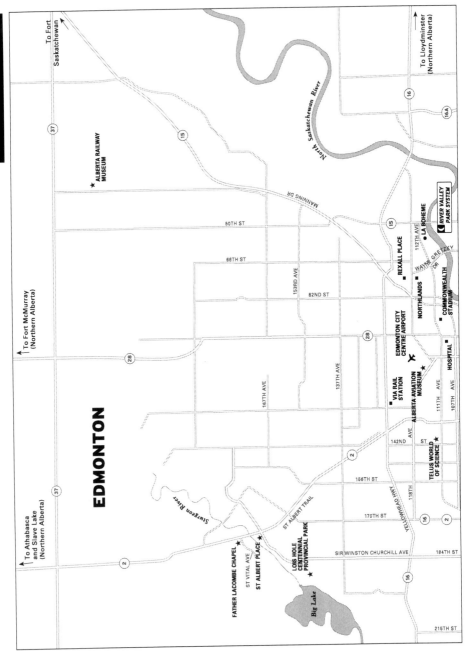

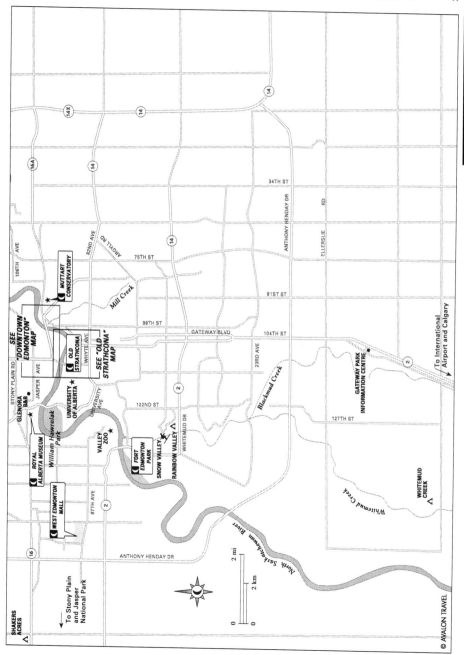

© AVALON TRAVEL

which crosses the North Saskatchewan River southwest of downtown. You can also head east along this ring road to access the northeast portion of the city. From the Anthony Henday intersection, Gateway Boulevard continues north to **Whitemud Drive,** an inner ring road providing access to Fort Edmonton Park, the zoo, and the mall, and then passes through **Old Strathcona,** crossing the North Saskatchewan River directly south of downtown.

The **Yellowhead Highway** passes through the city east to west, north of downtown. To get downtown from the east, take 97th Street. From downtown, Jasper Avenue changes to Stony Plain Road as it heads west, eventually joining Highway 16 at the city's western limits.

Since the early 1900s, Edmonton streets have been numbered. Avenues run east to west, numbered from 1st Avenue in the south to 259th Avenue in the north. Streets run north to south, numbered from 1st Street in the east to 231st Street in the west. Even-numbered addresses are on the north sides of the avenues and west sides of the streets. The center of the city is crossed by both 101st Street and 101st Avenue, the latter having retained its original name of **Jasper Avenue.**

When vast outlying areas were annexed by the city in 1982, new additions had to be made to the street-numbering system. First Street was renamed Meridian Street, and 1st Avenue was renamed Quadrant Avenue. The entire existing city now lies within the northwest quadrant, allowing for easy numbering of new streets as the city grows to the south and east.

PLANNING YOUR TIME

Edmonton is the perfect place to soak up city-type attractions, which makes a stop here an ideal way to break up your Alberta adventure. You can zip through the highlights in a single day, but that somewhat defeats the purpose of a break from an otherwise outdoorsy vacation. Instead, plan to spend at least one night in the capital, spoiling yourself at an upscale accommodation (the Union Bank Inn if a central location is important, the Varscona for a boutique splurge, or the Fantasyland Hotel if you have kids) and dining at one of the city's many fine restaurants. Regardless of your interests, **West Edmonton Mall** is the one attraction you won't want to miss. Even if shopping malls are not your idea of a vacation, the sheer excess of it all is an unforgettable eye-opener. In order of importance, plan on also visiting the **Royal Alberta Museum, Fort Edmonton Park,** and **Muttart Conservatory.** Visits to these four main attractions should fill a day and a half, leaving time to explore the historic **Old Strathcona** precinct and get back to nature in the **River Valley Park System** on foot or on a bike.

HISTORY

For at least 3,000 years, natives came to the river valley where Edmonton now stands, searching for quartzite to make stone tools. They had no knowledge of, or use for, the vast underground resources that would eventually cause a city to rise from the wilderness.

Fort Edmonton

European fur traders, canoeing along the North Saskatchewan River, found the area where Edmonton now stands to be one of the richest fur-bearing areas on the continent. Large populations of beavers and muskrats lived in the surrounding spruce, poplar, and aspen forest. In 1795, William Tomison, a Scotsman, built a sturdy log building beside the North West Company's Fort Augustus. He named it Fort Edmonton after an estate owned by Sir James Winter Lake, deputy governor of the Hudson's Bay Company. Both forts stood on the site of the present legislature-building grounds. It was an ideal location for trading. Cree and Assiniboine could trade beaver, otter, and marten pelts in safety, without encroaching on the territory of fierce Plains Indians, such as the Blackfoot. Yet the fort was far enough south to be within range of the Blackfoot—peaceable when outside their own territory—who came north to buy muskrat, buffalo meat, and other natural resources, which they later traded with Europeans.

After 100 years, the fur trade ended abruptly. Many of the posts throughout the West were abandoned, but Edmonton continued to be an important stop on the route north. Goods were taken overland from Edmonton to Athabasca Landing, where they were transferred to barges or steamers and taken north on the Athabasca River. Around this time, there was an increased demand for grains, and improving technology made agriculture more viable. This opportunity attracted settlers, who arrived through the 1880s to farm the surrounding land. Edmonton suffered a setback when the Canadian Pacific Railway (CPR) chose a southerly route through Calgary for the Transcontinental Railway. A branch built by the Calgary and Edmonton Railway Company arrived in 1891, but it ended on the south side of the North Saskatchewan River, at Strathcona.

The Klondike Gold Rush

The most common images of the Klondike Gold Rush in the Yukon are of miners climbing the Chilkoot or White Pass Trails in a desperate attempt to reach Dawson City. Often, for financial reasons, various other routes were promoted as being superior. The merchants of Edmonton led a patriot cry to try the "All-Canadian Route," which would allow prospectors to buy their supplies in a Canadian city rather than in Seattle. The proposed route followed the Athabasca Landing Trail north to Athabasca, continued by boat down the Athabasca, Slave, and Mackenzie Rivers to just south of the Mackenzie Delta, and ended with a short overland trip to the goldfields. The route was impractical and very difficult. Approximately 1,600 people were persuaded to attempt the route. Of these, 50 died, many turned back, and only 700 reached the Yukon. None reached the goldfields before 1899, when the main rush was over, and few, if any, found gold. This slim connection to the gold rush is now celebrated in the annual **Edmonton's Klondike Days.**

Selecting the Capital

The provinces of Alberta and Saskatchewan were both inaugurated on September 1, 1905. Because Regina had been the capital of the Northwest Territories, it was only natural that it continue as the capital of Saskatchewan. The decision about Alberta's capital did not come as easily, however. The Alberta Act made Edmonton the temporary capital, but it had plenty of competition. Other contenders were Athabasca Landing, Banff, Calgary, Cochrane, Lacombe, Red Deer, Vegreville, and Wetaskiwin. Each town thought it had a rightful claim: Banff because it could be fortified if war ever broke out, Vegreville for the clean air and a climate free of chinook winds. But the strongest claims were from the citizens of Calgary, who believed their city to be the financial and transportation center of the province. Heated debates on the subject took place in the Canadian capital of Ottawa and among rival newspaper editors, but Edmonton has remained the capital to this day. In 1912, Edmonton merged with Strathcona, giving the city a total population of 55,000. For the next 35 years, the city grew and declined according to the fortunes of agriculture.

Oil and a Growing City

Fur was Edmonton's first industry, and coal was its second. Commercial coal-mining operations began as early as 1880, with mining concentrated in three areas of the city. The last of more than 150 operations closed in 1970, and much of the coal seam remains unmined below the downtown area. But Edmonton's future lay not in coal, but oil. Since the discovery of "black gold" in 1947 at nearby Leduc, Edmonton has been one of Canada's fastest-growing cities. The building of pipelines and refineries created many jobs, and the city became the center of western Canada's petrochemical industry. As demand continued to rise, hundreds of wildcat wells were drilled around Edmonton. Farmers' fields were filled with derricks, valves, and oil tanks, and by 1956, more than 3,000 producing wells were pumping within 100 kilometers (62 miles) of the city.

Edmonton experienced the same postwar

boom of most major North American cities, as a major population shift from rural areas to the city began. By 1956, Edmonton's population had grown to 254,800, doubling in size since 1946. A 20-square-kilometer (eight-square-mile) area east of the city was filled with huge oil tanks, refineries, and petrochemical plants. Changes were also taking place within the city as the wealth of the oil boom began to take hold. Restaurants improved, and cultural life flourished. The city's businesses were jazzed up, and the expanding business community began moving into the glass-and-steel skyscrapers that form the city skyline today. Various service industries also became important; West Edmonton Mall alone employs 23,500 people.

2000 and Beyond

Although the original boom is over, oil is still a major part of the city's economy. Planned developments in the surrounding oil patch service area total approximately $40 billion in the first decade of the 21st century, with Edmonton benefiting directly from spin-off infrastructure. A great deal of this development is associated with the **oil sands** of Fort McMurray, including four "upgraders" costing $2.5 billion each that are currently under construction within city limits. In addition to oil-related companies, Edmonton's low cost of living is attractive to many companies. Economic Development Edmonton (www.ede.org) is a city-sponsored department that promotes the city to the world. One of its innovations is the sprawling **Edmonton Research Park,** on the southern outskirts, which has become a focal point for up-and-coming information technology and science companies. Nanotechnology is also big news in Edmonton, with the University of Alberta leading the way in research of material many thousands of times smaller than a human hair.

Sights

DOWNTOWN

Looking at Edmonton's dynamic skyline, it's hard to believe that not much more than 100 years ago the main drag was lined with dingy saloons and rowdy dance halls. Since those heady days, the city has seen many ups and downs—its present look is a legacy of the 1970s oil boom. The well-planned city center, on the northern bank of the North Saskatchewan River, is a conglomeration of skyscrapers that seemingly rose overnight when oil money flooded the city. The downtown core is fairly compact and is within walking distance of many hotels and the bus depot. **Jasper Avenue** (101st Avenue) is downtown's main thoroughfare, lined with restaurants and shops. At the east end of Jasper Avenue is the **Shaw Conference Centre,** a glass-and-steel building that appears to cling to the wall of the river valley. One block north is the large and popular **City Centre** shopping complex. On 102nd Street is the 36-story ManuLife Place, Edmonton's tallest building. A few blocks east is the **Arts District,** comprising the provincial government buildings, including the futuristic city hall, and an array of performing arts centers. (The streets immediately east of 97th Street are a skid row with sleazy bars—not the place to linger at night.)

Throughout all of the development, several historic buildings managed to survive. Many can be seen along **Heritage Trail,** a route taken by early fur traders that linked the old town to Fort Edmonton. Today the trail begins at the Shaw Conference Centre, at the corner of Jasper Avenue and 97th Street, and ends at the legislature grounds. The route is easy to follow—the sidewalk is paved with red bricks and lined with period benches, replica lampposts, and old-fashioned street signs.

Arts District

This complex, in the heart of downtown, occupies six square blocks and is one of the city's showcases. Within its limits are the Stanley

THE PEDWAY SYSTEM

The pedway system is unique and necessary this far north. It's a complex system of enclosed walkways linking office buildings, hotels, plazas, the civic center, and public transportation stops. Using the pedways, you can get virtually anywhere downtown without ever having to step outside into the elements. At first it all seems a bit complicated, but if you're armed with a map, the system soon becomes second nature. Pedways are below, above, or at street level, and the excellent signage makes it easy to find your way. The walkways are spotlessly clean, well lit, and relatively safe, although you wouldn't want to loiter around the Central Light Rail Transit (LRT) Station at night.

A. Milner Library, the Art Gallery of Alberta, Sir Winston Churchill Square, City Hall, the Law Courts Building, the Shaw Conference Centre, and the performing arts community's pride and joy, the magnificent Citadel Theatre and adjacent Winspear Centre.

Opened in early 2010, the futuristic **Art Gallery of Alberta** (northeast of Sir Winston Churchill Square on 99th St., 780/427-6223, 10:30 A.M.–5 P.M. Mon.–Wed. and Fri., 10:30 A.M.–8 P.M. Thurs., and 11 A.M.–5 P.M. Sat.–Sun., adult $10, senior $7, child $5) is an impressive 7,900-square-meter (85,000-square-foot) facility fronted by giant swirling steel curves representing the northern lights. It houses an extensive collection of 4,000 modern Canadian paintings as well as historical and contemporary art in all media. Various traveling exhibitions are presented throughout the year. The gallery also houses a theater, gift shop, and café.

City Hall (1 Sir Winston Churchill Square, 780/442-5311, 7 A.M.–10 P.M. Mon.–Fri., 9 A.M.–5 P.M. Sat.–Sun., free) built on the site of the old city hall, is designed to be the centerpiece of civic buildings within the Arts

District. The main public areas are ___ the main floor. Self-guided tours a__ during open hours. Immediately behind this area is the City Room, the building's main focal point. Its ceiling is a glass pyramid that rises eight stories. To the east are displays cataloging the city's short but colorful history.

Chinatown

An elaborate gateway designed by a master architect from China welcomes visitors to where Edmonton's small Chinatown *used* to be. The gate spans 23 meters (75 feet) across 102nd Avenue (also known as Harbin Road) at 97th Street. Eight steel columns painted the traditional Chinese color of red support it. Stretched across the center of the arch's roof is a row of ornamental tiles featuring two dragons, the symbol of power in China. The 11,000 tiles used in the gate were each handcrafted and glazed in China. In the last few years, Chinatown has moved up the road a few blocks. The archway now leads into an area of cheap boardinghouses and deserted parking lots but forms a colorful break from the pawnshops of 97th Street.

Fairmont Hotel MacDonald

This hotel (10065 100th St., 780/424-5181, www.fairmont.com/MacDonald) overlooking the river valley has long been regarded as Edmonton's premier luxury accommodation. For many years, it was the social center of the city. It was built in 1915 by the Grand Trunk Railway in the same château style used for many of the Canadian Pacific hotels across the country. After it closed in 1983, plans to tear it down were aborted; $28 million was spent on refurbishing it, and the hotel reopened, as grand and elegant as ever. The main lobby has been totally restored and opens to the Confederation Lounge and the Library, a bar overlooking the river that has the feel of an Edwardian gentleman's club. Ask at the reception desk for a map of the hotel.

Edmonton Public Schools Archives and Museum

Built in 1904, **McKay Avenue School** (on

EDMON

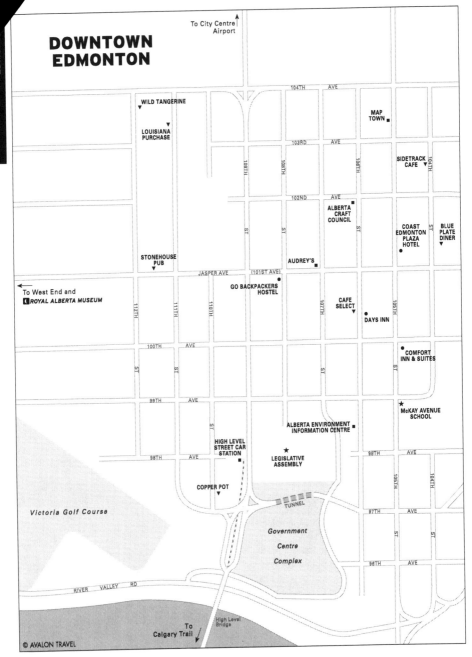

DOWNTOWN
EDMONTON

To City Centre
Airport

WILD TANGERINE

MAP
TOWN

104TH   AVE

LOUISIANA
PURCHASE

103RD   AVE

SIDETRACK
CAFE

102ND   AVE

ALBERTA
CRAFT
COUNCIL

COAST
EDMONTON
PLAZA
HOTEL

BLUE
PLATE
DINER

STONEHOUSE
PUB

AUDREY'S

JASPER AVE   (101ST AVE)

GO BACKPACKERS
HOSTEL

To West End and
ROYAL ALBERTA MUSEUM

CAFE
SELECT

DAYS INN

100TH   AVE

COMFORT
INN & SUITES

99TH   AVE

McKAY AVENUE
SCHOOL

ALBERTA ENVIRONMENT
INFORMATION CENTRE

HIGH LEVEL
STREET CAR
STATION

98TH   AVE

98TH   AVE

LEGISLATIVE
ASSEMBLY

COPPER POT

97TH   AVE

TUNNEL

Victoria Golf Course

Government

Centre

Complex

98TH   AVE

RIVER   VALLEY   RD

To
Calgary Trail

High Level
Bridge

© AVALON TRAVEL

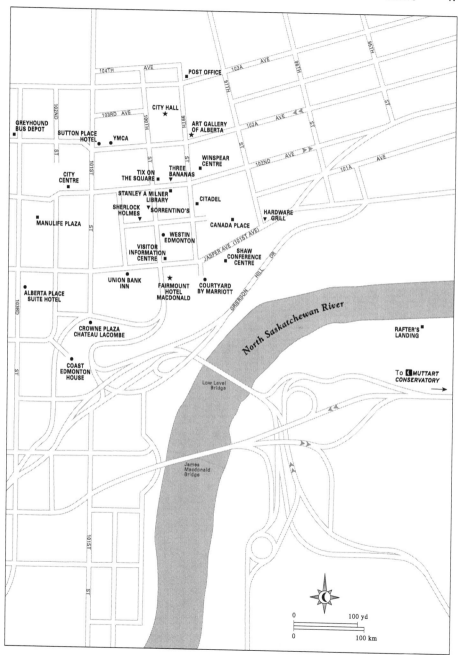

POST OFFICE

104TH AVE
103A AVE

CITY HALL ★
103RD AVE

GREYHOUND
BUS DEPOT

ART GALLERY
OF ALBERTA ★

102ND ST

SUTTON PLACE
HOTEL   YMCA

102A AVE

102ND AVE

WINSPEAR
CENTRE

101A AVE

CITY
CENTRE

101 ST

TIX ON
THE SQUARE

THREE
BANANAS

STANLEY A MILNER
LIBRARY

CITADEL

SHERLOCK
HOLMES   SORRENTINO'S

HARDWARE
GRILL

MANULIFE PLAZA

CANADA PLACE

WESTIN
EDMONTON

JASPER AVE (101ST AVE)

VISITOR
INFORMATION
CENTRE

SHAW
CONFERENCE
CENTRE

UNION BANK
INN

FAIRMOUNT
HOTEL
MACDONALD

COURTYARD
BY MARRIOTT

GRIERSON HILL DR

ALBERTA PLACE
SUITE HOTEL

North Saskatchewan River

RAFTER'S
LANDING

CROWNE PLAZA
CHATEAU LACOMBE

COAST
EDMONTON
HOUSE

To ◖MUTTART
CONSERVATORY
→

Low Level
Bridge

James
Macdonald
Bridge

101 ST

0   100 yd

0   100 km

the Heritage Trail, 10425 99th Ave., 780/422-1970, free) is Edmonton's oldest standing brick schoolhouse. It was the venue of the first two sittings of the provincial legislature in 1906. The building contains reconstructions of early classrooms and of the historic legislature assembly. Edmonton's first schoolhouse, a single-story wooden building dating to 1881, lies in back of the grounds, looking much as it would have to 19th-century students. It's open the same hours as early students attended, 12:30–4 P.M. Tuesday–Friday, as well as 1–4 P.M. Sunday.

Alberta Legislature Building

Home of the provincial government, this elegant Edwardian building (107th St. and 97th Ave.) overlooking the North Saskatchewan River Valley is surrounded by 24 hectares (59 acres) of formal gardens and manicured lawns. It officially opened in 1912 and, for many years, stood beside the original Fort Edmonton. Today it is one of western Canada's best examples of architecture from that era. Its 16-story vaulted dome is one of Edmonton's most

recognizable landmarks. Many materials used in its construction were imported: sandstone from near Calgary; granite from Vancouver; marble from Quebec, Pennsylvania, and Italy; and mahogany from Belize. The interior features a wide marble staircase that leads from the spacious rotunda in the lobby to the chamber and is surrounded by stained-glass windows and bronze statues.

Immediately north of the legislature building, beyond the fountains, is the **Legislative Assembly Interpretive Centre** (10820 98th Ave., 780/427-7362), which recounts the development of Alberta's political history and serves as the starting point for free tours of the legislature building. Tours depart daily on the hour in the morning from 9 A.M. and every 30 minutes in the afternoon weekdays until 5 P.M. mid-May–October, hourly 9 A.M.–4 P.M. weekdays and noon–4 P.M. weekends the rest of the year.

High Level Bridge

This bridge crosses the North Saskatchewan River at the bottom end of 109th Street. It

Alberta Legislature Building

© ANDREW HEMPSTEAD

EDMONTON

© ANDREW HEMPSTEAD

High Level Bridge

was built in 1913, linking the new capital to Strathcona. The bridge is 775 meters (2,500 feet) long and 53 meters (180 feet) above the river. It has been used as a tramway, a railway, a sidewalk, and a roadway. The rail line was in use until 1951, but in 2000 a local historical society began running a scheduled streetcar over the bridge. It runs from adjacent to the Grandin Light Rail Transit (LRT) Station across the bridge to as far south as Old Strathcona. The service, which costs $4 one-way, operates 45 minutes past the hour 11 A.M.–4 P.M. Sunday–Friday, 9 A.M.–4 P.M. Saturday mid-May–August 15.

In 1980, the **Great Divide Waterfall** was added to the bridge. When turned on, a curtain of water higher than Niagara Falls cascades down along the entire length of the bridge. It usually operates during special events such as Capital Ex, Canada Day, and on Sundays of long summer weekends.

Telephone Historical Centre

This museum (10440 108th Ave., 780/433-1010, 10 A.M.–3 P.M. Tues.–Thurs., donation)

catalogs the history of telecommunications in Edmonton from the introduction of telephones in 1885 to the present. It has many hands-on exhibits, including an early switchboard where you can make your own connections. Current technology is also displayed with exhibits of digital switching, fiber-optic cables, a talking robot, and cellular phones. A multimedia presentation in the small Alex Taylor Theatre traces telecommunications technology from its earliest days.

Ukrainian Sights

The **Ukrainian Canadian Archives and Museum** (9543 110th Ave., 780/424-7580, 10 A.M.–5 P.M. Tues.–Fri., noon–5 P.M. Sat., donation) exhibits artifacts from the lives of Ukrainian pioneers in Canada and has one of the largest archives in the country. Edmonton has 80,000 Canadians of Ukrainian descent, and as a result the city is home to a number of Ukrainian churches. One of the most impressive is **St. Josaphat's Ukrainian Catholic Cathedral** (97th St. at 108th Ave.), which is well worth a look for its elaborate decorations and pastel wall paintings.

SOUTHSIDE
◖ Muttart Conservatory

Nestled in the valley on the south side of the North Saskatchewan River are four large pyramid-shaped greenhouses that make up the Muttart Conservatory (9626 96A St. off 98th Ave., 780/442-5311, www.muttartconservatory.ca, 9:30 A.M.–5:30 P.M. Mon.–Fri., 11 A.M.–5:30 P.M. Sat.–Sun., adult $9.75, senior $7.25, child $5). Three of the greenhouses contain the flora of specific climates. In the arid pyramid are cacti and other hardy plants found in desertlike conditions. The tropical pyramid holds a humid jungle, one of North America's largest orchid collections, and colorful and raucous exotic birds, who live among the palms. The temperate pyramid features plant species from four continents, none of which would grow naturally in Edmonton's harsh environment. The contents of the fourth pyramid change with the season but always feature colorful floral displays such as red, white, and yellow poinsettias at Christmastime. Take bus number 85 or 86 south along 100th Street to get to the conservatory.

Edmonton Queen

The *Edmonton Queen* is a 52-meter (170-foot) paddle wheeler that cruises along the North Saskatchewan River from Rafter's Landing (9734 98th Ave., 780/424-2628), near Muttart Conservatory. One-hour cruises depart at noon and 3 P.M. Friday–Sunday late May–mid-September (adult $18, child under 11 $12, lunch extra), and evening cruises depart at 7:30 P.M. (adult $48, child under 11 $22, including dinner). To get to Rafter's Landing, take 98th Avenue east along the south side of the river.

John Walter Museum

This historic site located near the Kinsmen Sports Centre consists of three houses—dating from 1875, 1884, and 1900—that were built by John Walter for his family. The first house was a stopping point for travelers using

Walter's ferry service to cross the river. Walter also opened a carriage works, a lumber mill, and a coal mine, and at one time even built a steamship. For a time, the area was known as Walterdale, but with the completion of the High Level Bridge, the need for a ferry service ended. Today, all that remains are Walter's houses. Each house holds exhibits corresponding to the period of its construction and depicts the growth of Edmonton and the importance of the North Saskatchewan River. The buildings are open only 1–4 P.M. Sunday February–December, with bread-making demonstrations, old-fashioned games, or some other related activity scheduled to correspond with these hours. Admission is free, and the grounds are pleasant to walk through at any time. The museum is at 10627 93rd Avenue. From downtown, take 101st Street south down Bellamy Hill and cross the river at the Walterdale Bridge. On foot, allow 30–60 minutes. By bus, jump aboard number 9 west along 102nd Avenue or number 52 from Old Strathcona. For further information, call 780/496-4852.

John Walter Museum

© ANDREW HEMPSTEAD

Rutherford House

Designated as a Provincial Historic Site, this elegant Edwardian mansion (11153 Saskatchewan Dr., 780/422-2697, 9 A.M.–5 P.M. daily in summer, noon–5 P.M. Tues.–Sun. the rest of the year) was built in 1911 for Alexander C. Rutherford, Alberta's first premier. The Rutherford family lived in this house for 30 years. It was then used as a University of Alberta fraternity house before being restored to its original condition and furnished with antiques from the Edwardian period. You can wander throughout the two-story house, but the highlight is the Arbour Restaurant, operating as a tearoom in summer (11:30 A.M.–4 P.M. Tues.–Sun.), serving lunch ($8–11) and afternoon tea ($7–22) using historical recipes from 1915 or earlier. It's on the University of Alberta campus. The easiest way to get there by public transport is on the LRT from downtown.

◀ Fort Edmonton Park

An authentic reconstruction of the early trading post from which Edmonton grew is only a small part of this exciting attraction (off Whitemud Dr. near Fox Dr., 780/496-8787, 10 A.M.–4 P.M. Mon.–Fri. and 10 A.M.–6 P.M. Sat.–Sun. May–June, 10 A.M.–6 P.M. daily July–Aug., 10 A.M.–4 P.M. daily Sept., adult $13.50, senior $10.25, child $6.75), Canada's largest historic park. From the entrance, a 1919 steam locomotive takes you through the park to the Hudson's Bay Company Fort, which has been built much as the original fort would have looked in 1846—right down to the methods of carpentry used in its construction. Step outside the fort and walk forward in time—to 1885 Street, re-creating downtown Edmonton between 1871 and 1891, when the West was opened up to settlers. The street is lined with wooden-facaded shops such as a bakery, a boat builder, a blacksmith, and a trading post. As you continue down the road, you round a corner and are on 1905 Street, in the time period 1892–1914, when the railway had arrived and Edmonton was proclaimed provincial capital. **Reed's Tea Room,** near the far end of the street, serves English teas and scones

noon–4 P.M. in a traditional atmosphere. By this time, you're nearly on 1920 Street, representing the years 1914–1929—a period of social changes when the business community was developing and the city's industrial base was expanding. Stop by Bill's Confectionary (noon–4 P.M.) for a soda or sundae, hitch a lift aboard the streetcar, or plan an overnight stay at the **Hotel Selkirk** to round out the roaring '20s experience.

What really makes this park come alive are the costumed interpreters, immersed in life as it was in Edmonton of days gone by—preparing cakes and pastries for sale at the bakery, tending to carefully re-created vegetable plots, making butter beside the farmhouse, giving piano lessons to interested passersby, or just getting together for a friendly game of horseshoes. In addition, a constant variety of scheduled activities is offered.

John Janzen Nature Centre

Beside Fort Edmonton Park (use the same parking lot) is John Janzen Nature Centre (780/496-2939, 9 A.M.–4 P.M. Mon.–Fri. year-round, longer hours and weekends in summer, adult $2, senior and child $1.65), which has hands-on exhibits, displays of local flora and fauna—both dead and alive—and a four-kilometer (2.5-mile) self-guided interpretive trail that leads through the river valley and loops back to the center. In one room, various natural environments have been simulated with displays of frogs, fish, snakes, salamanders, and a working beehive made from glass. Throughout the year, special events are held, films are shown, and Sunday nature walks are conducted.

Valley Zoo

Across the river from Fort Edmonton Park is the city zoo (end of Buena Vista Rd., off 142nd St., 780/496-6911, 9:30 A.M.–6 P.M. daily May–Aug., 9:30 A.M.–4 P.M. daily the rest of the year, adult $9.75, senior $7.25, child $5), which holds approximately 350 animals, representing all seven continents. It is designed mainly for kids, with a petting zoo, camel and pony rides, paddleboats, a miniature train, and cut-out storybook characters. To get there by bus, take number 12 west along 102nd Avenue to Buena Vista Road and walk 1.6 kilometers (one mile) down to the park. On summer Sundays, bus number 200 leaves on the hour from the University Transit Centre and goes right to the zoo.

◖ OLD STRATHCONA

When the Calgary and Edmonton Railway Company completed a rail line between the province's two largest cities, it decided to end it south of the North Saskatchewan River and establish a town site there, rather than build a bridge and end the line in Edmonton. The town was named Strathcona, and it grew to a population of 7,500 before merging with Edmonton in 1912. Because of an early fire-prevention bylaw, buildings were built of brick. Today many still remain, looking much as they did at the turn of the 20th century. Old Strathcona is Edmonton's best-preserved historic district. In addition to the old brick buildings, the area has been refurbished with brick sidewalks and replica lampposts. The commercial core of Old Strathcona is centered along Whyte (82nd) Avenue west of the rail line. More than 75 residential houses built before 1926 are scattered to the north and west of Whyte Avenue.

Across from the rail line is the **Strathcona Hotel** (corner of 103rd St. and Whyte Ave.), one of the few wood-framed buildings surviving from the pre-1900 period. Before Strathcona had permanent churches, congregations worshipped in the hotel, and during Prohibition it was used as a ladies' college. The two blocks east of the hotel are lined with cafés and restaurants, used bookstores, and many interesting shops. One of Old Strathcona's oldest businesses is the 1910 **Hub Cigar and Newsstand** (8116 Gateway Blvd., 780/439-0144), just off Whyte Avenue, which stocks more than 10,000 different newspapers and magazines from around the world. In a converted bus garage one block north of Whyte Avenue is the **Old Strathcona Farmer's Market** (10310 83rd Ave., 780/439-1844, 8 A.M.–3 P.M. Sat. year-

round), with plenty of fresh produce, crafts, and homemade goodies for sale.

The best way to get to Old Strathcona from downtown is aboard the **High Level Street Car** (780/437-7721), which runs from the west side of the Alberta Legislature Building to the 104th Street and 85th Avenue intersection in Old Strathcona. It departs downtown 15 and 45 minutes past the hour 11 A.M.–4 P.M. Sunday–Friday and 9 A.M.–4 P.M. Saturday mid-May–August, $4 one-way. From the station, wander south to bustling Whyte Avenue.

Many of the historic buildings have plaques at street level, but the brochures *A Walk Through Old Strathcona* and *Historical Walking and Driving Tour: Strathcona* make a stroll much more interesting. For more information on the district, contact the **Old Strathcona Foundation** (780/433-5866, www.oldstrathconafoundation.ca).

C&E Railway Station Museum

Strathcona's original railway station was located just north of the CPR station. It was later moved farther along the line, then demolished and replaced with a replica that houses a railway museum. The museum (10447 86th Ave., 780/433-9739, 10 A.M.–4 P.M. Tues.–Sat. in summer, donation) relives the days of steam engines and settlers, when people streamed into the newly opened Canadian West from around the world.

WEST OF DOWNTOWN

From the city center, Jasper Avenue (101st Avenue) goes west through the **West End**—where many residential and commercial buildings date from the boom years of 1912–1914—and continues to **Glenora,** one of the city's oldest and most sought-after neighborhoods. Many streets are lined with elegant two-story mansions from the early 1900s. The neighborhood fountain in Alexander Circle (103rd Avenue and 133rd Street) is the center of the area.

◖ Royal Alberta Museum

The provincial museum (12845 102nd Ave.,

OLD STRATHCONA

DA-DE-O

105TH ST

JULIO'S BARRIO MEXICAN RESTAURANT

104TH ST

WHYTE AVE (82ND AVE)

WEE BOOK INN

STRATHCONA HOTEL

103RD ST

102ND ST

BLOCK 1912

SHERLOCK HOLMES PUB

PRINCESS THEATRE

HUB CIGAR AND NEWSSTAND

GREENWOOD'S

0   50 yds

0   50 m

0   200 yds

0   200 m

North

High Level Bridge

Saskatchewan

Waltardale Bridge

River

SASKATCHEWAN DR

JOHN WALTER MUSEUM

RUTHERFORD HOUSE

Waterdale Park

KINSMEN SPORTS CENTRE

University Of Alberta

Queen Elizabeth Park

87TH AVE

112TH ST

86TH AVE

YARDBIRD SUITE

C&E RAILWAY MUSEUM

103TH ST

85TH AVE

HIGH LEVEL STREET CAR STATION

110TH ST

108TH ST

106TH ST

105TH ST

104TH ST

101ST ST

84TH AVE

111TH ST

109TH ST

107TH ST

83ND AVE

WALTERDALE PLAYHOUSE

FARMER'S MARKET

102ND ST

MUDDY WATERS

O'BYRNE'S IRISH PUB

THE VARSCONA

SEE DETAIL

TRACK AND TRAIL

MANDARIN RESTAURANT

WHYTE AVE (82ND AVE)

EDMONTON BOOKSTORE

To The Unheardof

81ST AVE

HI-EDMONTON

COOK COUNTY SALOON

ALHAMBRA BOOKS

© AVALON TRAVEL

)0, 9 A.M.–5 P.M. daily, adult $10, child $5) overlooks the river valley in the historic neighborhood of Glenora. It is one of Canada's largest (18,800 square meters/200,000 square feet) and most popular museums. Exhibits catalog one billion years of natural and human history. The highlight is most definitely the **Wild Alberta Gallery,** where a water setting and the province's four natural regions—mountain, prairie, parkland, and boreal forest—are re-created with incredible accuracy. Lifelike dioramas are only part of the appeal. Much of the exhibit encourages visitor interaction to solve the mystery of what is Alberta's most dangerous mammal, to touch the teeth of a grizzly bear, or soak up the sound of a bull moose calling in the female members of his species.

Elsewhere in the museum, the Natural History Gallery explains the forces that have shaped Alberta's land, describes the dinosaurs of the Cretaceous period and mammals of the ice age (such as the woolly mammoth), and displays a large collection of rocks and gems. Another section, the Syncrude Gallery of Aboriginal Culture, details Alberta's indigenous peoples, from their arrival 11,000 years ago to the way in which their traditions live on today through thousands of artifacts, Aboriginal interpreters, and audiovisual presentations. Other sections tell the story of the province's earliest explorers and the settlers who came from around the world to eke out a living in the harsh environment. The Bug Room, another favorite, displays insects dead and alive from around the world. The museum is well known for hosting traveling exhibits, making repeat visits worthwhile. The museum also has a gift shop and a café. To get there, take bus number 100 along Jasper Avenue.

In front of the museum is **Government House** (780/427-2281, tours 11 A.M.–4:30 P.M. Sun. in summer, free), an impressive three-story sandstone structure built in 1913 for Alberta's lieutenant governor, who would entertain guests in the lavish reception rooms or in the surrounding gardens. The building was later used as a hospital, and then restored to its former glory in the 1970s.

Alberta Aviation Museum

This museum, adjoining Edmonton City Centre Airport (11410 Kingsway Ave., 780/451-1175, 10 A.M.–6 P.M. Mon.–Fri., 10 A.M.–4 P.M. Sat.–Sun., adult $9, senior $7, child $5), dates to World War II, when the hangars held British aircraft involved in training programs. Today the hangars contain 27 restored aircraft, including a favorite of early Canadian bush pilots—the Fairchild 71-C. One of the most recently completed projects was the on-site restoration of a World War II de Havilland Mosquito.

Telus World of Science

Completed in 1984, this multipurpose complex (11211 142nd St., 780/452-9100, 10 A.M.–5 P.M. daily, until 9 P.M. in summer) in Coronation Park is one of Edmonton's major attractions and most recognizable landmarks. Displays are spread over three levels and six galleries. They include a look into the future of communications; the chance to solve a crime along Mystery Avenue; the Robotics Lab; a ham radio station hooked up to similar stations around the world; a weather display that includes an audiovisual of the deadly tornado that hit Edmonton in the summer of 1987; a tribute to Royal Canadian Mounted Police (RCMP); the **Margaret Zeidler Star Theatre,** where laser light shows are presented noon–7 P.M. daily with a different show each hour; an interactive Eye-lusions exhibit; a chance to learn about the environment in Green's House; exploration of the human body in the Body Fantastic Gallery; Discoveryland, especially for kids; a room with 20 computer terminals linked to the Internet; and Sport II, which gives you the chance to try your hand at a variety of sports, including wheelchair racing.

A day pass (adult $14, senior $12, child $9.50) includes admission to all of the above galleries and theater presentations. Also in the building, an **IMAX Theatre** presents spectacular video productions—seemingly always of an

Half price admission Sat & Sun for 9–11am

interesting nature—projected onto a 13-by-19-meter (43-by-62-foot) screen; adult $14, senior $12, child $9.50 for the theater only; $22.50, $19, and $15.25, respectively, for admission to one IMAX feature and the other displays.

Beside the complex is an **observatory,** which is open to the public 1–5 P.M. daily, then 7–10 P.M. (weather permitting) for star-, moon-, and planet-gazing; no charge.

By bus from downtown, take number 125 west along Jasper Avenue to Westmount Station and hoof it through Coronation Park.

◖ WEST EDMONTON MALL

Feel like a trip to the beach to do some sunbathing and surfing? Would you like to play a round of golf? How about launching from the world's only indoor bungee jump? Do you like eating at Parisian cafés? Does watching a National Hockey League team in training seem like a good way to spend the afternoon? Do the kids like sea lion shows? And at the end of the day, would you like to sink into a hot tub, surrounded by a lush tropical forest? All of these activities are possible under one roof at West Edmonton Mall, the largest shopping and indoor amusement complex in the whole world. Calgary may have the greatest *outdoor* show on earth, but Edmonton has what can surely be billed as the greatest *indoor* show on earth, a place that is visited by 22 million people annually. Much more than an oversized shopping mall, Edmonton's top tourist attraction is a shop-and-play four-season wonderland, where many visitors check into the 355-room luxury Fantasyland Hotel, stay a weekend, and never set foot outside the mall's 58 entrances.

WEST EDMONTON MALL

90TH AVE

PARKING

MAIN LEVEL

SEARS

GALAXYLAND
AMUSEMENT
PARK

MINI
GOLF

BOURBON STREET

GUEST
SERVICES

178TH ST

Deep Sea
Adventure

ICE
PALACE

INFORMATION
BOOTH

170TH ST

THE BAY

FANTASYLAND
HOTEL

World
Waterpark

PARKING

TRANSIT
STATION

PARKING

ZELLERS

87TH AVE

SCALE NOT AVAILABLE

© AVALON TRAVEL

WEST EDMONTON MALL TRIVIA

WEST EDMONTON MALL IS:

• the world's largest shopping and amusement complex, encompassing 483,000 square meters (5.3 million square feet) – that's equivalent to 115 football fields

WEST EDMONTON MALL HAS:

• over 800 stores

• over 100 eateries

• 58 entrances

• 21 movie screens

• 325,000 light bulbs

• five postal codes

• the world's largest parking lot (parking for 20,000 vehicles)

• the world's largest indoor amusement park

• the world's largest water park, covering two hectares (five acres) and containing 12.3 million liters (2.7 million gallons) of water

• the world's largest indoor lake (122 meters/400 feet long)

• the world's tallest indoor bungee jump

WEST EDMONTON MALL:

• cost over $1 billion to construct

• employs 23,500 people

• uses the same amount of power as a city of 50,000

• attracts 22 million people a year (over 60,000 per day)

Shopping is only one part of the mall's universal appeal. Prices are no less than anywhere else in the city, but the experience of having more than 800 stores (including more than 200 womenswear stores, 35 menswear stores, and 55 shoe shops) under one roof is unique.

Aside from the shops, many other major attractions fill the mall. **Galaxyland Amusement Park** is the world's largest indoor amusement park, with 25 rides, including Mindbender—a 14-story, triple-loop roller coaster (the world's largest indoor roller coaster)—and Space Shot, a 13-story, heart-pounding free fall. Off to one side, Galaxy Kids Playpark offers the younger generation the same thrills and spills in a colorful, fun-loving atmosphere. Admission is free, but the rides cost money. A Galaxyland day pass, allowing unlimited rides, is adult $31.95, families $84.95, senior or those under 1.2 meters (four feet) $24.95.

In the two-hectare (five-acre) **World Waterpark,** you almost feel as though you're at the beach: the temperature is a balmy 30°C (85°F), and a long sandy beach (with special nonslip sand), tropical palms, colorful cabanas, a beach bar, and waves crashing on the shore all simulate the real thing. The computerized wave pool holds 12.3 million liters (2.7 million gallons) of water and is programmed by computer to eject "sets" of waves at regular intervals. Behind the beach are 22 waterslides that rise to a height of 26 meters (85 feet). The World Waterpark also has the world's only indoor bungee jump, **Center for Gravity** (780/489-4339, $75), three whirlpools, and a volleyball court. On the second floor of the mall is a water-park viewpoint. Admission to World Waterpark is adult $31.95, families $84.95, senior or those under 1.2 meters (four feet) $24.95.

At the same end of the mall as World Waterpark is the world's largest indoor lake. Here, you can gawk at the area along its entire 122-meter (400-foot) length from either the main or second floor of the mall. The most dominant feature of the lagoon is a full-size replica of Christopher Columbus's flagship, the *Santa Maria*. It was built in False Creek, Vancouver, and shipped across the Rockies to its new indoor home. You can jump aboard a bumper boat ($4 for five minutes); descend into the depths of the **Sea Life Caverns** ($5.95 per person) to view sharks, penguins, and a variety of colorful fish; or take a scuba-diving course.

Other major attractions in the mall include **Professor WEM's Adventure Golf** (adult $10, senior and child $7) and, smack in the middle of the mall, the **Ice Palace.** This NHL-size skating rink is the second home of the Edmonton Oilers, who occasionally practice here. It's open to the public year-round; adult $8 per session, senior or child $6, skate rental $4.

Other sights include an aviary with various exotic birds, a Chinese pagoda that was hand-carved by four generations of the same family, replicas of the British crown jewels, bronze statues commissioned especially for the mall, and a couple of aquariums. Three theme streets—**Europa Boulevard, Chinatown,** and the glitzy New Orleans–style **Bourbon Street**—hold some of the mall's 100 restaurants and eateries.

Hours and Other Practicalities

Shopping hours vary seasonally but are generally 10 A.M.–9 P.M. Monday–Saturday, noon–6 P.M. Sunday. Hours of the various attractions and restaurants vary. Many restaurants stay open later, and the nightclubs stay open to the early hours of the morning.

Mall maps color-code each of four phases to make finding your way around easier (shops and attractions use a phase number as part of their address). Maps are widely available throughout the mall. The two official information centers are both on the main level near the Ice Palace—a booth on the east side and Guest Services north toward Entrance 8. Staff will answer all commonly asked questions, while the tech-savvy can download a Mobile Mall Map to their Palm PDA; both are open regular shopping hours. When your legs tire, **scooter rentals** are available near the information booth; $6 for the first hour, $4 for each additional hour. For more information, contact West Edmonton Mall at 780/444-5200, www.westedmontonmall.com.

The mall is on 170th Street, between 87th and 90th Avenues. Parking is usually not a problem, but finding your car again can be, so remember which of the 58 entrances you parked near (a parking lot along 90th Avenue at 175th Street is designated for RVs). From downtown, take bus number 100.

DEVON
Devonian Botanic Garden

These gardens (780/987-3054, 10 A.M.–6 P.M. Mon.–Wed. and 10 A.M.–8 P.M. Thurs.–Sun. July–Aug., 10 A.M.–5 P.M. daily May and Sept., adult $13, senior $8.50, child $5), developed by the University of Alberta, are located southwest of the city and five kilometers (3.1 miles) north of the small town of Devon, which was named for the Devonian rock formation in which nearby oil strikes were made during the late 1940s. The 70-hectare (173-acre) site has been developed around the natural contours of the land. The highlight is the **Kurimoto Japanese Garden,** one of the world's northernmost authentic Japanese gardens. The various natural elements are complemented by an ornamental gate, an arched bridge, and decorative lanterns. Other features are the large Alpine Garden, with examples of plants from mountainous regions; the Herb Garden, where in August the aroma is almost overpowering; the Peony Collection, which is at its most colorful in July; a greenhouse filled with plants unique to the Southern Hemisphere; and the Native People's Garden, which is surrounded by water and showcases plants used by the native people of Alberta.

STONY PLAIN
Multicultural Heritage Centre

West of Edmonton, the streets of Stony Plain, which was homesteaded before 1900, are lined with historic buildings, but the best place to learn more about the community's history is at this Provincial Historic Site (5411 51st St., 780/963-2777, 10 A.M.–4 P.M. daily, free). On the grounds, the town's first high school houses a museum, a craft store, a library and archives, a candy store, and the **Heritage Kitchen**—a basement restaurant serving pioneer-style home-cooked meals at reasonable prices. Housed next door, in the historic residence of an early pioneer, is **Oppertshauser House,** Alberta's first rural public art gallery.

ST. ALBERT

The city of St. Albert (pop. 59,000)—northwest of Edmonton along the St. Albert Trail—is one of Alberta's oldest settlements but has today become part of Edmonton's sprawl. Albert Lacombe, a pioneering western Canadian priest, built a mansion overlooking the Sturgeon River in 1861, when Fort Edmonton was only a small trading post. A sawmill and gristmill were constructed, and by 1870, St. Albert was the largest agricultural community west of Winnipeg. Father Lacombe's first log

chapel, the **Father Lacombe Chapel** (west of Hwy. 2 on St. Vital Ave., 780/459-7663, 10 A.M.–6 P.M. daily mid-May–Aug., adult $2, senior and child $1.50), was built in 1861 and had a brick structure built around it in 1927. Now a Provincial Historical Site, it has been restored to its original appearance. Beside the chapel, a cast-iron statue of Father Lacombe that was made in France overlooks the city. Also on Mission Hill is the **Vital Grandin Centre,** an imposing three-story structure built in 1887 as a hospital.

In stark contrast to the historic buildings overlooking the Sturgeon River is City Hall in **St. Albert Place** on St. Anne Street, a contoured brick building designed by Douglas Cardinal. Inside is the **Musée Heritage Museum** (780/459-1528, 10 A.M.–5 P.M. Tues.–Sat., 1–5 P.M. Sun., donation), with displays

---

FATHER ALBERT LACOMBE

Dressed in a tattered black robe and brandishing a cross, Father Albert Lacombe, known to natives as "the man with the good heart," dedicated his life to those with native blood – the Assiniboine, Blackfoot, Cree, and, in particular, the Métis. His travels, mainly associated with northern Alberta, took him as far south as Calgary, but his reputation extended to every corner of the province. He was a spokesman for the church, an effective influence on government policies, and, most importantly, he had a hand in just about every advance in the often-tense relationship between warring tribes and white men.

Father Lacombe originally came to what is now Alberta in 1852 to serve the Métis and natives who had moved to Fort Edmonton. In his time there he founded missions at what are now St. Albert and Brosseau. After a short stint in Manitoba, he returned as a traveling missionary, establishing Canada's first industrial school for natives. He also mediated a dispute between the Canadian Pacific Railway and angry leaders of the Blackfoot over rights to build a rail line through a reserve, and he wrote the first Cree dictionary. The trust he

built with native leaders was great; during one rebellion of the Blackfoot Confederacy, it is claimed that his influence prevented the slaughter of every white man on the prairies.

FATHER LACOMBE, O.M.I.
A MISSIONARY   UN MISSIONNAIRE
& PIONEER   & PIONNIER
OF THE NORTHWEST.   DU NORD-OUEST.

© ANDREW HEMPSTEAD

telling the story of St. Albert's history and the people who made it happen. From this museum, walk along the river (3 km/1.9 miles) or drive (take Sir Winston Churchill Avenue to Riel Drive) to **Lois Hole Centennial Provincial Park,** protecting Big Lake and surrounding wetlands. Here, bird-watchers have the chance to see some 40 species of water and wading birds, including trumpeter swans.

St. Albert Information Centre (71 St. Albert Rd., 780/459-1724, 8 A.M.–5 P.M. Mon.–Fri., 10 A.M.–5 P.M. Sat.–Sun.) is in a large modern building beside Highway 2 on the south side of St. Albert (you can't miss it coming into the city from the south).

FORT SASKATCHEWAN AND VICINITY

In 1875—long after the fur-trading post of Fort Edmonton had been established—the North West Mounted Police (NWMP) marched north from Fort Macleod and established its northern divisional fort on the North Saskatchewan River, 30 kilometers (18.6 miles) northeast of Fort Edmonton. In the ensuing years, Fort Saskatchewan has grown into a large residential center, right at Edmonton's doorstep. To reach the town, take Highway 15 (Manning Drive) out of Edmonton.

Peter T. Ream Historic Park

This park protects the site of the original Fort Saskatchewan overlooking the river from along 101st Street in downtown Fort Saskatchewan. A jail and courthouse replaced the original fort in 1909. The jail was demolished in 1994, but the two-story, redbrick courthouse still stands and now serves as a museum (10006 100th Ave., 780/998-1783, 10 A.M.–4 P.M. Mon.–Fri., adult $5, senior $4, child $3) cataloging the history of the site and the NWMP. Various other historic buildings have been moved to this picturesque site, including a restored log homestead, a blacksmith shop, and a one-room schoolhouse. A cairn marking the site of the NWMP guard room has been built from stones used in the original structure.

Alberta Railway Museum

If antique railway memorabilia interests you, consider stopping at this museum (24215 34th St., 780/472-6229, 10 A.M.–5 P.M. Sat.–Sun. mid-May–Aug., adult $5, senior $3.50, child $2), a short detour from Highway 15 to Fort Saskatchewan. Or take 97th Street (Highway 28) north to Namao, turn east on Highway 37 and travel seven kilometers (4.3 miles), then go south on 34th Street for two kilometers (1.2 miles). It is well signposted from both directions. Featuring Canada's largest collection of Northern Alberta Railway (NAR) equipment, this museum also has rolling stock from the Canadian National Railway (CNR) and the CPR. More than 50 locomotive, passenger, and freight cars from 1877 to 1950 are displayed, some fully restored, others in the process of being so. Also exhibited are various railway artifacts, equipment, machinery, and the simple one-room flag-stop shelter from the rural hamlet of Opal.

Sports and Recreation

◖ RIVER VALLEY PARK SYSTEM

One of the first things you'll notice about Edmonton is its large amount of parkland. The city has more land set aside for parks, per capita, than any other city in Canada. Most parks interconnect along the banks of the North Saskatchewan River and in adjoining ravines, encompassing 7,400 hectares (18,300 acres) and comprising the largest stretch of urban parkland in North America. Within these parks are picnic areas, swimming pools, historic sites, golf courses, and many kilometers of walking and biking trails. One of the best ways to ensure you make the most of the park system is by referring to the brochure *Priceless Fun,* available from tourist information centers and online at the City of Edmonton website (www.edmonton.ca).

One of the larger individual parks is **William Hawrelak Park,** west of the university along Groat Road. A one-way road loops through the park, circling a man-made lake with paddle-boats and fishing. There are many quiet picnic areas and an outdoor amphitheater that hosts a wide range of summer events.

SWIMMING AND FITNESS CENTERS

It's often crowded, it's commercial, and it's not cheap, but Edmonton's ultimate swimming, sliding, and sunbathing experience awaits at **World Waterpark** in the West Edmonton Mall (170th St. and 87th Ave., 780/444-5200, adult $29.95, families $79.95, child under 1.2 meters/four feet $22.95).

Edmonton's outdoor swimming season lasts approximately three months beginning at the end of May. Of the five outdoor pools owned by the city, the one in **Queen Elizabeth Park** is in a particularly picturesque location among poplar trees and with a view of the city skyline over the river; access is from 90th Avenue. Another pool, close to the city center, is in **Mill Creek Park,** north of Whyte Avenue (82nd Avenue) on 95A Street. Admission to all outdoor pools is $4.

When the weather gets cooler, or to take advantage of more facilities, head to one of the city's many indoor pools, where admission includes the use of saunas, a hot tub, weight rooms, and waterslides. Swimming events of the 1978 Commonwealth Games were held at the **Kinsmen Sports Centre** (9100 Walterdale Hill, 780/944-7400), in Kinsmen Park on the south bank of the North Saskatchewan River. Admission (adult $8, senior $6, child $4) includes use of the pools, fitness center, sauna, and jogging track. The cafeteria here has reasonably priced meals.

GOLF

Edmonton has so many golf courses that you could play a different one each day for a month. One is within a three-iron shot of the city center, whereas others are along the North

RedTail Landing golf course

© ANDREW HEMPSTEAD

Saskatchewan River Valley and throughout outlying suburbs. Canada's oldest municipal course is the **Victoria Golf Course** (west of the legislature building along River Rd., 780/496-4710, $38–46), which is still owned and operated by the city. This 18-hole course is only a little more than 6,000 yards in length but is made challenging by narrow fairways and smallish greens.

As an enthusiastic golfer, I can highly recommend the following courses that have opened in the last decade: 7,330-yard **RedTail Landing** (Hwy. 2 by the airport, 780/890-7888, $95), a links-style layout with well-placed bunkers and multiple water hazards, and **Jagare Ridge** (14931 9th Ave., 780/432-4030, $90), stretching along both sides of the Whitemud Creek Valley. West of the city, **The Ranch** (52516 Range Rd., Spruce Grove, 780/470-4700, $75) features a water-lined trio of finishing holes (and carts equipped with GPS and electronic scoring).

TOURS

If you are pressed for time, or even if you're not, a guided tour of Edmonton may be a good idea. The big tour companies bypass Edmonton, leaving a variety of small operators to offer personalized service and flexible schedules. As you'd expect from a former museum guide, Cameron Malcolm of **Out an' About Tours** (780/909-8687, www.out-anabouttours.com) emphasizes the heritage and culture of Edmonton and Old Strathcona on his half-day Alberta Past & Present Tour city tours ($65), with the option to add a visit to Fort Edmonton Park ($75). **Magic Times** (780/940-7479, www.magictimes.ca) takes interested visitors on tours that concentrate on one area, such as Old Strathcona, or historic sites and Fort Edmonton Park. Expect to pay around $60 per person for a four-hour tour. Wayne Millar of **Watchable Wildlife Tours** (780/405-4880, www.birdsandbackcountry. com) leads visitors through regional parks, with his forte the areas east of Edmonton, including Elk Island National Park (three-hour evening tour is $79) and the Cooking Lake Moraine; tours leave on demand.

WINTER RECREATION
Downhill Skiing and Snowboarding

The closest major alpine resort is Marmot Basin, in Jasper National Park, but Edmonton has three small lift-serviced hills within the city limits and one just outside. All are great for beginners but won't hold the interest of other skiers or snowboarders for very long. Overlooking downtown from across the river is the **Edmonton Ski Club** (9613 96th Ave., 780/465-0852). It's open December–March, with night skiing during the week. Lift tickets are adult $25, child $19, which includes use of a small terrain park. To get there, follow signs to the Muttart Conservatory. Also close to the city center is **Snow Valley** (southwest of downtown, where Whitemud Dr. crosses the river, 780/434-3991), which has a chairlift, a T-bar, and a small terrain park. Tickets are around the same price as the ski club.

Cross-Country Skiing

The River Valley Park System provides ample opportunity for cross-country skiing. More than 75 kilometers (47 miles) of trails are groomed December–early March. The most popular areas are in William Hawrelak Park, up Mill Creek Ravine, and through Capilano Park. For details of trails, pick up the brochure *Cross-Country Ski Edmonton* from tourist information centers, or download it from the City of Edmonton website (www.edmonton.ca). The **Kinsmen Sports Centre** has cross-country ski rentals; $15 for two hours, or $24 per day, including boots and poles.

SPECTATOR SPORTS
Hockey

Alberta's first major-league hockey team was the Alberta Oilers, who played in both Calgary and Edmonton. The team finally settled in Edmonton permanently for the 1973–1974 season. During the 1980s, when Wayne Gretzky was leading the **Edmonton Oilers,** the NHL's Stanley Cup resided just as permanently in Edmonton, "City of Champions." Since 1988, when Gretzky was sold to the L.A. Kings, the team has met with mixed success, although they did reach the Stanley Cup final in 2006. Home games are played September–April in Rexall Place (Wayne Gretzky Dr., 780/414-4625 or 866/414-4625, www.edmontonoilers.com). From downtown, the easiest way to get there is by LRT to the Coliseum station. Tickets cost from $55 and go all the way up to $235 for rink-side seats.

Football

The **Edmonton Eskimos** have a distinguished record in the Canadian Football League (CFL), having won the Grey Cup 13 times—including five straight (1978–1982) and most recently in 2005. "Eskimos" was originally an insult, given to the team by a Calgary sportswriter in the team's early days, but the name stuck. Since 1948, the team has played in and won more Grey Cup games than any other team in the league. Two former Albertan premiers, Peter Lougheed and Don Getty, once starred for the team. The "Esks" play late June–November at Commonwealth Stadium (11000 Stadium Rd., 780/448-3757 or 800/667-3757, www.esks.com). Tickets are $35–65, with children half price.

Horse Racing

Harness racing takes place at **Northlands** (7300 116th Ave., 780/471-7210, www.northlands.com) spring–mid-December. Thoroughbred racing takes place throughout summer at the same track. Racing is generally at 6 P.M. on Friday and at 1 P.M. on weekends. During Capital Ex celebrations, a full racing program is presented. Admission is nominal.

Entertainment and Events

For details on theater events throughout the city, a listing of art galleries, what's going on where in the music scene, cinema screenings, and a full listing of festivals and events, pick up a free copy of *See Magazine* (www.seemagazine.com) or *Vue Weekly* (www.vueweekly.com). Both are published every Thursday and are available all around town, with all the same information presented on the respective websites. Tickets to most major performances are available from **Tix on the Square** (Sir Winston Churchill Square, 9930 102nd Ave., 780/420-1757, www.tixonthesquare.ca, 9:30 A.M.–6 P.M. Mon.–Fri., 9:30 A.M.–4 P.M. Sat.), a nonprofit outlet operated by the local arts council.

THE ARTS
Art Galleries

Scattered throughout the city are commercial art galleries, many of which exhibit and sell Canadian and native art. Eight galleries within six blocks of each other and the corner of Jasper Avenue and 124th Street have formed the **Gallery Walk Association of Edmonton** (www.gallery-walk.com). All are worth visiting, but the **Bearclaw Gallery** (10403 124th St., 780/482-1204) is of special note for those searching out the unique art of the First Nations. Among the shoe shops and souvenir stands in West Edmonton Mall is **Northern Images** (780/444-1995), also with a good collection of native and northern arts and crafts. Finally, headquarters for the **Alberta Craft Council** is the Edmonton store (10186 106th St., 780/488-6611).

Theater

Edmonton's 14 theater companies present productions at various locations all year long. For most companies, September–May is the main season.

The **Citadel** (9828 101A Ave., 780/425-1820 or 888/425-1820, www.citadeltheatre.com) is Canada's largest theater facility, taking up an entire downtown block. From the outside, it looks like a gigantic greenhouse; one entire side is glass, enclosing a magnificent indoor garden complete with walking paths and benches. The complex houses five theaters: the

Maclab Theatre showcases the work of teens and children; the intimate Rice Theatre features mainly experimental and innovative productions; Zeidler Hall hosts films, lectures, and children's theater; Tucker Amphitheatre presents concerts and recitals across a pond and surrounded by tropical greenery, and often puts on small lunchtime stage productions; and Shoctor Theatre is the main stage for the Citadel's long-running subscription program ($28–65 per production). Tickets are available from the Citadel Box Office.

For slightly more adventurous productions and occasional international imports, see what's going on at the **Northern Light Theatre** (11516 103rd St., 780/471-1586, www.northernlighttheatre.com, $20). Edmonton's oldest theater is the **Walterdale Playhouse** (10322 83rd Ave., 780/439-2845, www.walterdaleplayhouse.com, from $8), in the heart of Old Strathcona, which presents historical and humorous material through an October–June season in a 1910 fire hall.

Jubilations Dinner Theatre (Upper Level Phase II, West Edmonton Mall, 780/484-2424 or 877/214-2424, $60–70) is a popular interactive dinner theater, combining music and comedy. Shows start at 6:30 P.M. Wednesday–Saturday and at 5 P.M. Sunday.

Music and Dance

In the heart of the Arts District is the magnificent **Winspear Centre** (corner of 99th St. and 102nd Ave., www.winspearcentre.com), a venue renowned as an acoustic wonder that is also capable of producing high-quality amplified sound. It is home to the **Edmonton Symphony Orchestra** (780/428-1108, www.edmontonsymphony.com) and attracts a wide variety of national and international musical acts, ranging from choirs to classical performers. Contact the box office (780/428-1414 or 800/563-5081, $29–48) for tickets.

Both the **Edmonton Opera** (780/429-1000, www.edmontonopera.com) and the **Alberta Ballet** (780/702-4725, www.albertaballet.com) perform at the Northern Alberta Jubilee Auditorium in the University of Alberta (11455

87th Ave.) October–March. For performance dates and ticket information, call the box office numbers or Ticketmaster (780/451-8000).

Cinemas

Cineplex cinemas are located throughout the city, including 10233 Jasper Avenue (780/428-1307); 2950 Calgary Trail S. (780/436-6977); and in West Edmonton Mall (780/444-2400). The historic **Magic Lantern Princess Theatre** (10337 82nd Ave., Old Strathcona, 780/433-0728) is an old-time movie house showing revivals, experiments, and foreign films. **Metro Cinema** (Zeidler Hall, The Citadel, 9828 101A Ave., 780/425-9212) shows classics, imports, and brave new films. The **Magic Lantern Garneau Theatre** (8712 109th St., 780/433-0728) features mostly foreign films and those that have gained acclaim at film festivals. Admission is generally $10, except Monday, when it's discounted to $5.

NIGHTLIFE
Casinos

Casinos in Alberta are all privately owned, but charitable organizations hold the actual gaming licenses (and keep the profits). Licenses allow slots to be turned on at 10 A.M. and table games to start at noon, with all the action coming to a close at 3 A.M. In addition to slots, the casinos offer blackjack, roulette, baccarat, Red Dog, and Sic Bo. The largest of Edmonton's casinos is the Western-themed **Casino Yellowhead** (Yellowhead Trail and 153rd St., 780/424-9467). **Palace Casino** (Phase II, West Edmonton Mall, 780/444-2112) has the advantage of location in tempting players to its tables.

Bars and Nightclubs

The **Sidetrack Cafe** (10238 104th St., 780/421-1326) is central to downtown, serves excellent food, and presents live entertainment nightly from 9 P.M. Shows change dramatically—one night it might be stand-up comedians, the next a blues band, then jazz—and the only thing you can rely on is that it will be busy. Monday is usually comedy night and

Sunday variety night. Cover charges vary; $5–10 is normal. Downtown, the **Sherlock Holmes** (10012 101A Ave., 780/426-7784) serves a large selection of British and Irish ales and is the place to head for St. Patrick's Day (March 17). The rest of the year, drinkers are encouraged to join in nightly sing-alongs with the pianist. Sherlock Holmes also has locations in Old Strathcona (10341 82nd Ave., 780/433-9676) and along West Edmonton Mall's Bourbon Street (780/444-1752). Old Strathcona is also home to **O'Byrne's Irish Pub** (10616 82nd Ave., 780/414-6766), where Celtic bands often play. The **Stonehouse Pub**, a few blocks west of downtown (11012 Jasper Ave., 780/420-0448), attracts an older crowd with classic rock-and-roll pumping from the jukebox. It has an outdoor patio, plenty of pool tables, big-screen TVs, and nightly drink specials.

The **Confederation Lounge** (Fairmont Hotel Macdonald, 10065 100th St., 780/424-5181) oozes old-time style, while **Bellamy's** (Crowne Plaza Chateau Lacombe, 10111 Bellamy Hill, 780/428-6611) is a quiet space with river views.

Cook County Saloon (8010 Gateway Blvd., 780/432-2665) is consistently voted Canada's Best Country Nightclub by the Canadian Country Music Association. Its mellow honky-tonk ambience draws crowds, and Canadian and international performers play here. Free two-step lessons are offered on selected weeknights, and on Friday and Saturday nights the action really cranks up, with live entertainment and a DJ spinning country Top 40 discs. On these two nights, the cover is $8 after 8 P.M. Beyond West Edmonton Mall is **Cowboys** (10102 180th St., 780/481-8739), with a Western theme but attracting a young, fratlike crowd with theme nights, popular promotions, white-hatted and scantily clad shooter girls, and a huge dance floor.

Top 40 and dance nightclubs change names, reputations, and locations regularly, but some are reliable fixtures. Even if the names change, the locations don't—Old Strathcona and West

Edmonton Mall both offer a range of nightclubbing experiences. Your best bet for finding current hot spots is Edmonton's free entertainment rags, *See Magazine* and *Vue Weekly,* or the website www.clubvibes.com.

Jazz and Comedy

The Edmonton Jazz Society is a volunteer-run organization that manages the **Yardbird Suite** (11 Tommy Banks Way., 780/432-0428, www.yardbirdsuite.com). Live jazz fills the air 10 P.M.–2 A.M. nightly September–June. Admission is $5–24. The **Full Moon Folk Club** (www.fmfc.org) sponsors visiting performers at a variety of venues, including St. Basil's Cultural Centre (10819 71st St.); tickets are well priced at approximately $18.

At **Yuk Yuk's Komedy Kabaret** (Century Casino, 13103 Fort Rd. NW, 780/481-9857, www.yukyuks.com), showtimes vary, but they offer at least one show nightly Wednesday–Saturday. Generally, Wednesday is amateur night, and the pros hit the stage Thursday–Saturday. Tickets are $5–19.

FESTIVALS AND EVENTS
Spring
The **International Children's Festival** (780/459-1542, www.childfest.com) takes place the weekend closest to June 1 in the Arden Theatre, St. Albert. Acts from around the world include theater, music, dance, storytelling, and puppetry.

The Works: Art & Design Festival (780/426-2122, www.theworks.ab.ca) features art exhibitions on the streets, in parks, and in art galleries through Old Strathcona for the last two weeks of June.

During the last week of June through to early June, the **Edmonton International Jazz Festival** (780/990-0222, www.edmontonjazz. com) is held at various indoor and outdoor venues, including the renowned Yardbird Suite. Many foreign stars make special appearances.

Summer
For 10 days in early July, downtown's

Winston Churchill Square comes alive during the **Edmonton International Street Performers Festival** (780/425-5162, www. edmontonstreetfest.com), with almost 1,000 performances by magicians, comics, jugglers, musicians, and mimes.

The 10-day **Capital Ex** (780/471-7210, www.capitalex.ca), beginning on the third Thursday of each July, kicks off with a massive parade through downtown. Much of the activity is centered on Northlands (7300 116th St.), featuring a midway; casino; free music concerts; gold panning; the Alberta Tattoo; the RCMP musical ride; thoroughbred racing; the Global Connections pavilion, featuring an international marketplace; and a trade show of upscale arts and crafts. This is the city's biggest annual event, attracting approximately 800,000 visitors, so be prepared for big crowds everywhere. Running in conjunction with Capital Ex is **Taste of Edmonton** (Sir Winston Churchill Square, 780/423-2822, www.eventsedmonton.ca), where visitors can sample signature dishes from Edmonton's wide range of restaurants.

Fifty outdoor ethnic pavilions at Hawrelak Park are just a small part of the **Heritage Festival** (780/488-3378, www.heritage-festival.com), which is held on the first weekend in August as a celebration of the city's multicultural roots. Visitors to the festival have the opportunity to experience international singing and dancing, arts-and-crafts displays, costumes, and cuisine from more than 60 cultures.

During the **Edmonton Folk Music Festival** (780/429-1999, www.edmontonfolkfest.org), held on the second weekend of August, Gallagher Park comes alive with the sound of blues, jazz, country, Celtic, traditional, and bluegrass music. Tickets are $55 per day,

although advance weekend passes are better value for eager folkies.

Quickly becoming one of the city's most popular events is the **Fringe Theatre Festival** (780/448-9000, www.fringetheatreadventures. ca), a 10-day extravaganza that begins on the second Thursday in August. It is held throughout Old Strathcona, in parks, on the streets, in parking garages, and in the area's historic restored theaters. With more than 1,000 performances and a crowd of half a million looking on, the festival has become North America's largest alternative-theater event, attracting artists from around the world. Tickets are generally inexpensive.

Symphony under the Sky (780/428-1414, www.edmontonsymphony.com), held on the weekend closest to August 31, is the last gasp in Edmonton's busy summer festival schedule. Led by the Edmonton Symphony Orchestra, this five-day extravaganza of classical music takes place in William Hawrelak Park.

Fall and Winter

Farmfair International (780/471-7210, www. farmfairinternational.com) showcases some of North America's best livestock through sales and auctions, but exhibits, a trade show, the judging of Miss Rodeo Canada, and thousands of farm animals draw in casual visitors. The fair takes place at Northlands the second week of November. That same week, Rexall Place hosts the **Canadian Finals Rodeo** (780/471-7210, www.canadianfinalsrodeo. com). This $500,000 event is the culmination of the year's work for Canada's top 10 money-earning cowboys and cowgirls in seven traditional rodeo events. The action takes place at 7 P.M. Wednesday–Saturday and 1 P.M. Saturday–Sunday.

Shopping

PLAZAS AND MALLS

Naturally, any talk of a shopping trip to Edmonton includes **West Edmonton Mall** (at 87th Ave. and 170th St., 780/444-5200, www.westedmontonmall.com), the world's largest shopping and amusement complex. Downtown's major shopping centers are **City Centre** and **ManuLife Place,** while on the southern outskirts **South Edmonton Common** (corner Gateway Blvd and 23rd Ave.) provides a home for 35 big box stores.

CAMPING GEAR AND WESTERN WEAR

Downtown, **Uniglobe Geo Travel** (10237 109th St., 780/424-8310) stocks a wide range of travel clothing and accessories, and also operates as a travel agency. **Mountain Equipment Co-op,** a Canadian outdoor equipment cooperative similar to REI in the United States, is west of the Royal Alberta Museum (12328 102nd Ave., 780/488-6614). Across the railway tracks from Old Strathcona is **Track 'n' Trail** (10148 82nd Ave., 780/432-1707), which carries a wide variety of cross-country skiing, camping, and climbing gear. In the same general area is **Totem Outdoor Outfitters** (7430 99th St., 780/432-1223), with more of the same, as well as kayaks, canoes, and some used gear. West of downtown is the large **Campers Village** (10951 170th St., 780/484-2700), with camping equipment, fishing tackle, books, boots, and scuba-diving equipment.

Alberta's largest supplier of Western wear is **Lammle's,** with five outlets throughout the city, including one in West Edmonton Mall

(Phase I, 780/444-7877). High-quality boots are also sold by **Diablo Boots** (3440 Gateway Blvd., 780/435-2592).

BOOKSTORES

Audrey's (10702 Jasper Ave., 780/423-3487, 9 A.M.–9 P.M. Mon.–Fri., 9:30 A.M.–5:30 P.M. Sat., noon–5 P.M. Sun.) has the city's largest collection of travel guides, western Canadiana, and general travel writing on two vast floors. **Map Town** (10344 105th St., 780/429-2600, 9 A.M.–5:30 P.M. Mon.–Fri., 10 A.M.–5 P.M. Sat.) stocks the provincial 1:50,000 and 1:250,000 topographical map series, along with city maps, world maps, Alberta wall maps, travel guides, atlases, and a huge selection of specialty maps. Map Town also has a solid selection of specialty guides for fishing, canoeing, climbing, and the like.

Old Strathcona is an excellent place for browsing through used bookstores. **Wee Book Inn** (10310 82nd Ave., 780/432-7230) is the largest and stocks more recent titles and a large collection of magazines. **Alhambra Books** (upstairs at 10115 81st Ave., 780/439-4195) specializes in Canadiana and has an extensive collection of Albertan material, pamphlets and newspapers. **Athabasca Books** (8228 105th St., 780/431-1776) stocks mostly history and literature books. The **Edmonton Bookstore** (10533 82nd Ave., 780/433-1781) has a large stock of out-of-print books from the region.

Old Strathcona's lone nonchain new-book store is **Greenwood's** (7925 104th St., 780/439-2005), which stocks a lot of everything.

Accommodations and Camping

Nearly all of Edmonton's best hotels are located downtown. Other concentrations of motels can be found along Gateway Boulevard (Highway 2 from the south) and scattered along Stony Plain Road in the west. The towns of Leduc and Nisku have several motels close to Edmonton International Airport. Other options include many bed-and-breakfasts, a centrally located hostel, and camping (just five minutes from downtown, or in campgrounds west, east, or south of the city).

DOWNTOWN

All but two of the following accommodations (Glenora B&B Inn and La Boheme are the exceptions) are within walking distance of each other within the downtown core. As with city hotels around the world, parking is extra ($8–15) but may be included with weekend rates.

Under $50

Housed in one of the few older downtown hotels to escape the wrecking ball is **Go Backpackers Hostel** (10815 Jasper Ave., 780/424-4146 or 877/646-7835, www.go-hostels.ca, dorm beds $25–28, $70–80 d), a few blocks from the heart of the city and surrounded by cafés, restaurants, and pubs. The hostelry has a total of 184 beds in eight- and four-bed dorms, as well as a few twin and double rooms. Facilities include two lounges, free wireless Internet, and a communal kitchen.

The **YMCA** has an outstanding location right downtown (10030 102A Ave., 780/421-9622, www.edmonton.ymca.ca, $40–43 s, $58–63 d). The rooms are small and sparsely furnished; each has a bed and desk, some have a sink, and the bathroom is down the hall. They are available to men, women, couples, and families. Downstairs is a café, and guests have free access to the center's fitness facility (including a pool).

$50-100

Between downtown and the Royal Alberta Museum, **Glenora B&B Inn** (12327 102nd Ave., 780/488-6766 or 877/453-6672, www.glenorabnb.com, $70–155 s, $90–175 d) is a home away from home a short walk from the galleries of 124th Street. The building that houses this bed-and-breakfast was built as a commercial enterprise in 1912 and has been completely renovated, with the guest rooms above a guest parlor and street-level restaurant where a full breakfast is served (included in rates). Even the least-expensive rooms have an en suite bathroom, or pay extra for Medium Suite, with basic cooking facilities. For the same price as a midpriced downtown hotel, upgrade to a spacious Apartment Suite, complete with a kitchenette, canopied bed, and oversized bathroom.

$100-150

Sure, it's a chain hotel, but **Comfort Inn & Suites** (10425 100th Ave., 780/423-5611 or 888/384-6835, www.comfortinnedmonton.com, $110–150 s or d) is a good choice. The 108 rooms are sensibly furnished for both leisure and business travelers. Parking, local calls, and in-room coffee are complimentary.

The **Days Inn** (10041 106th St., 780/423-1925 or 800/267-2191, www.daysinn.com, from $119 s or d) is another solid choice in the same neighborhood. Parking and wireless Internet are free. The in-house restaurant is open 6:30 A.M.–9 P.M., and a lounge stays open until midnight.

No, it's not downtown, but it's close. **La Boheme** (6427 112th Ave., 780/474-5693, www.laboheme.ca, $125 s, $155 d) is in the historic Gibbard building, which originally held Edmonton's first luxury apartments. Today, La Boheme restaurant downstairs is one of the city's best, and six upstairs rooms have been graciously refurnished and are run as a bed-and-breakfast. The building is certainly charming, right down to its creaky floors. Each of the simply furnished rooms has a separate sleeping area. Rates include a continental breakfast.

If you plan to be in the city for a few days

EDMONTON

and want to cook your own meals, suite hotels (also called apartment hotels) offer a good value. **Alberta Place Suite Hotel** (10049 103rd St., 780/423-1565 or 800/661-3982, www.albertaplace.com, $112–179 s or d) is one of the best choices. The 84 suites are large, and each has a well-equipped kitchen. Continental breakfast, parking, and daily papers are complimentary; a Hertz agent is on-site (discounted rentals for guests); and Jasper Avenue is only half a block away.

Coast Edmonton House (10205 100th Ave., 780/420-4000 or 800/716-6199, www. coasthotels.com, $140–265 s or d) is slightly more expensive than Alberta Place, but each of the 303 rooms has a balcony with views of the valley or the city, and there's an indoor pool, a fitness room, and a guest lounge and reading room.

Renovated in 1998, the 24-story **Crowne Plaza Chateau Lacombe** (10111 Bellamy Hill, 780/428-6611 or 800/661-8801, www. chateaulacombe.com, $129–229 s or d) sits on Bellamy Hill, and its unusual cylindrical design distinguishes it against the skyline. The Chateau Lacombe features 307 guest rooms, a fitness center, gift shop, a bar with river views, and a revolving restaurant that actually has decent food. Upgrades to the suites are reasonable and worth the extra money.

$150-200

If you're looking for accommodations in this price category, it's very hard to do better than the **Union Bank Inn** (10053 Jasper Ave., 780/423-3600 or 888/423-3601, www.union-bankinn.com, $199–349 s or d) for value, charm, and location. The inn is in a restored 1911 bank building in the heart of the city. The owners have transformed the historic building into a luxurious boutique hotel, featuring a fireplace, down comforters, and bathrobes in each of 34 tastefully decorated rooms spread through two themed wings (heritage and contemporary). The rates include a cooked breakfast, a wine-and-cheese tray presented to guests each evening, and free parking 3 P.M.–9 A.M.

Centrally located on the corner of Jasper Avenue and 99th Street, the **Courtyard by Marriott** (1 Thornton Court, 780/423-9999 or 866/441-7591, www.marriott.com, $169 s or d) is a modern and unpretentious hotel with spectacular views across the river valley. The 177 rooms that fill with natural light (or none at all if you close the heavy curtains) have plenty of space and big, modern bathrooms. Downstairs is a bistro with tables that spill onto a magnificent riverside patio.

The lobby of the **Coast Edmonton Plaza Hotel** (10155 105th St., 780/423-4811 or 800/716-6199, www.coasthotels.com, $169–189 s or d) has a distinct alpine feel, yet the rest of the property is nothing but city-style. Handsome rooms come with niceties—such as robes—that make you believe you're paying more than you are. You can pay more, for a Superior Room, and it will be money well spent. Facilities include an indoor pool, an exercise room, laundry service, a lounge, and a restaurant. Disregard the rack rates (a quick check of the hotel website uncovered a $139 bed-and-breakfast package for two that included parking—in July!). At $10 per 24 hours, parking is well priced compared to other downtown hotels.

Over $200

The **Fairmont Hotel Macdonald** (10065 100th St., 780/424-5181 or 800/441-1414, www.fairmont.com, from $229 s or d) is an Edmonton landmark that was originally part of the Canadian Pacific hotel chain (along with the Palliser Hotel in Calgary and the Banff Springs Hotel in Banff) but is now part of the Fairmont Hotels and Resorts chain. The 199 guest rooms come in several configurations (many are on the small side). A subtle air of old-world European elegance extends throughout the rooms and public areas, such as the upscale restaurant and the beautiful lounge overlooking the river valley.

Joined to the pedway system and very central, but still affording great river views, is the 20-story **Westin Edmonton** (10135 100th St., 780/426-3636 or 800/228-3000, www. thewestinedmonton.com, $249–329 s or d), one the city's best hotels. The 416 rooms are large, luxurious, and come with all the comforts of home. Hotel facilities include a large indoor pool and a fitness center. The in-house eatery, Pradera, is a stylish space that spills into the cavernous lobby. While the Westin rooms and facilities are all excellent, this hotel gets the nod as a Top Pick for its discounted online rates, which are often under $100.

It's upscale all the way at the **Sutton Place Hotel** (10235 101st St., 780/428-7111 or 866/378-8866, www.suttonplace.com, $319–459 s or d), in the financial district and linked to other buildings by the pedway system. In each of the 313 elegantly furnished rooms you'll find marble tabletops, walnut furniture, brass trimmings, a large work area, and a bay window. Other hotel facilities include an indoor pool, an exercise room, a lounge, and a restaurant notable for its well-priced breakfast buffet ($18) and flavor-filled menu of local specialties. Join this company's loyalty program to receive free wireless Internet and discounted in-house dining.

SOUTH OF DOWNTOWN

Gateway Boulevard, an extension of Highway 2 as it enters the city from the south, offers a few cheap roadside motels just beyond Gateway Park, and is then dotted with chain hotels all the way to Old Strathcona. Remember when looking at addresses along this strip that Gateway Boulevard is Highway 2 northbound and Calgary Trail is Highway 2 southbound.

Under $50

HI-Edmonton (10647 81st Ave., 780/988-6836 or 866/762-4122, www.hihostels.ca) is sensibly located within walking distance of the hippest Edmonton neighborhood, Old Strathcona, with the best choice of restaurants, bars, and nightclubs. The building may seem a little clinical at first, but that feeling goes away when you begin to take advantage of the facilities offered. The lounge area is spacious and comfortable, and there's a quiet and private backyard, plenty of space in the kitchen, and off-street parking. Throughout summer,

various trips and barbecues are put on, and a desk is set up in the lounge to take bookings for local sights and recreation. Most rooms are two-bed dorms ($31.50 per night for members of Hostelling International, $35.50 for nonmembers), but there are a few rooms with five or six beds ($28 and $32 respectively) and private rooms, some with en suites ($89 s, $99 d). Check-in is after 3 P.M. From the Greyhound bus depot, walk two blocks east to 101st Street and catch the number 4, 6, 7, or 9 bus south. Get off at 82nd Avenue, then walk two blocks east and one south, and you're there.

$50-100

At the southern city limits, **Chateau Motel** (1414 Calgary Trail SW, 780/988-6661, $60–69 s, $69–89 d) has easy access to the airport, and each room has a microwave and fridge.

Over $150

As you drive north along Gateway Boulevard, it's impossible to miss the 11-story, pastel-colored **Delta Edmonton South** (4404 Gateway Blvd., 780/434-6415 or 800/268-1133, www.deltahotels.com, $189 s or d) towering over the major intersection with Whitemud Drive. Guests are offered a wide variety of facilities and services, including an indoor pool, a renovated restaurant, a lounge, an airport shuttle, and valet parking.

Adjacent to the Delta is the **Radisson Hotel Edmonton South** (4440 Gateway Blvd., 780/437-6010 or 888/333-3333, www.radisson.com, from $169 s or d), another 200-plus-room, full-service hotel centered on a greenery-filled atrium.

One of the city's finest accommodations is ◖ **The Varscona,** situated in the heart of Old Strathcona (8208 106th St., 780/434-6111 or 866/465-8150, www.varscona.com, from $180 s or d). The Varscona experience combines the personalized atmosphere of a boutique hotel with all the amenities you'd expect of an upscale chain. The 89 guest rooms are spacious and elegantly furnished in one of three pleasing styles. They all have

EDMONTON

© ANDREW HEMPSTEAD

Hotel Selkirk

king beds, large bathrooms, and niceties such as bathrobes and gourmet in-room coffee. Casual Murrieta's is the Varscona's contribution to Old Strathcona's vibrant dining scene, while O'Byrne's Irish Pub is the place to relax with a pint. Parking, a light breakfast, a daily newspaper, and an evening wine-and-cheese-tasting session are included.

Look no further than the (**Hotel Selkirk** (780/496-7227 or 877/496-7227, www.hotelselkirk.com, mid-May–Aug., $185–235 s or d) for a unique overnight experience with a historic twist. The original Hotel Selkirk along Jasper Avenue burnt down in 1962, but the historic property has been re-created in minute detail in Fort Edmonton Park, off Whitemud Drive southwest of downtown. The guest rooms have a cozy, Victorian feel but enjoy modern conveniences such as air-conditioning and Internet connections. Meal and accommodation packages are inclusive of breakfast and dinner in the downstairs Johnson's Café. Drinks in the Mahogany Room, at a replica of Canada's longest bar, are extra.

WEST EDMONTON
$50-100

If you're on a budget and want to stay out by the mall, consider the 149-room **Yellowhead Inn** (5 km/3.1 miles away at 15004 Yellowhead Trail, 780/447-2400 or 800/661-6993, www.yellowheadinn.com, $79 d, $89 d), across from a casino and with an in-house restaurant and lounge.

Slightly more expensive, the next nearest accommodation is the three-story **West Harvest Inn** (17803 Stony Plain Rd., 780/484-8000 or 888/882-9378, www.westharvest.ca, $99 s or d), offering 160 well-appointed air-conditioned rooms and a free mall shuttle.

$100-150

The pick within a cluster of choices along Stony Plain Road, a five-minute drive from the mall, is the **Sandman Hotel West Edmonton** (17635 Stony Plain Rd., 780/483-1385 or 800/726-3626, www.sandman.ca, $139–169 s or d). The rooms are handsomely appointed in sharp tones and comfortable furnishings. The central atrium holds a pool and restaurant—a pleasant respite from the busy road out front. The suites here are super-spacious.

$150-200

West Edmonton Mall Inn (17504 90th Ave., 780/444-9378 or 800/737-3783, www.westedmontonmall.com, $169 s, $189 d) lies across the road from its namesake. It features 88 well-appointed rooms, each with two comfortable beds, a coffeemaker, and a Sony PlayStation. Check the website for packages that include mall activities.

Over $200

Within West Edmonton Mall is the 355-room (**Fantasyland Hotel** (17700 87th Ave., 780/444-3000 or 800/737-3783, www.fantasylandhotel.com, $249–449 s or d), famous for elaborately themed rooms that are way over the top. The hotel has over 100 themed rooms, as well as 230 regular rooms and a few extremely spacious Executive Suites with jetted tubs, and three restaurants. But it's the theme rooms that this hotel is known for. No catching a cab back to your hotel after a day of shopping here—just ride the elevator to the room of your wildest fantasy. Each floor has a theme; the choice is yours: Hollywood, Roman, Polynesian, Victorian, African, Arabian, Igloo, Water Park, Western, Canadian Rail, or Truck (where you can slumber in the bed of a real pickup truck). Each theme is carried out in minute detail. The Polynesian room fantasy, for example, begins as you walk along a hallway lined with murals depicting a tropical beach, floored with grass matting. You'll walk through a grove of palm trees before reaching your room. In the colorful room, an enormous hot tub is nestled in a rocky grotto, and the bed is shaped like a warrior's catamaran, with a sail as the headboard. This escapism comes at a cost, but maybe not as much as you'd expect—rack rates start at $349 s or d, but outside of the busiest summer weekends, rates are reduced, and often passes to mall attractions are included.

CAMPGROUNDS
South

The best camping within the city limits is at the **Rainbow Valley Campground** (13204 45th Ave., 780/434-5531 or 888/434-3991, www.rainbow-valley.com, mid-Apr.–mid-Oct., tent sites $26, powered sites $30). The location is excellent, and, as far as city camping goes, the setting is pleasant. Facilities include free showers, a laundry room, a barbecue grill, a playground, and a cooking shelter. In summer, all sites are full by noon, so reserve ahead by credit card. To get there, turn south off Whitemud Drive at 119th Street, then take the first right and follow it into the valley.

If you're coming into the city from the south, take Ellerslie Road west from Highway 2 to access **Whitemud Creek Golf and RV Resort** (3428 156th St., 780/988-6800, www.whitemudcreek.com, $45). The 125 fully serviced sites are bunched together in the middle of a full-length, nine-hole golf course ($35), which is adjacent to a pleasant little creek. Facilities include a stocked trout pond, modern washrooms, a laundry room, and a clubhouse

restaurant. To get there, follow Ellerslie Road three kilometers (1.9 miles) west from Highway 2, then take 127th Street for three kilometers (1.9 miles) south, then 40th Avenue west for a similar distance.

In the town of Devon, a 20-minute drive southwest of the city, is **River Valley Lions Campground** (1140 Saskatchewan Ave. E., 780/987-4777, www.devonlionspark.com, May–mid-Oct., $21–36), which lies alongside the North Saskatchewan River and beside a golf course. To get there from Highway 2, take Highway 19 west; from out near West Edmonton Mall, take Highway 60 south from Highway 16.

West

Continue west from West Edmonton Mall to **Shakers Acres** (21530 103rd Ave., 780/447-3564 or 877/447-3924, www.shakersacresrvpark.com, $31–38), on the north side of Stony Plain Road. Facilities include a laundry, Wi-Fi, a playground, and a convenience store.

Farther out, in Spruce Grove, is the **Glowing Embers Travel Centre** (26309 Hwy. 16, 780/962-8100 or 877/785-7275, www.glowingembersrvpark.com, Apr.–Oct., $38–45), with over 280 sites. All facilities are modern, and although tents are allowed, they may look out of place among the satellite-toting RVs. Facilities include a recreation hall, a grocery store, Wi-Fi, a restaurant (breakfast and lunch only), an RV wash, a launderette, and service bays with licensed technicians on hand.

East

Half Moon Lake Resort (21524 Hwy. 520, 780/922-3045, www.halfmoonlakeresort.ca, tents $35, hookups $38–42) is on the shore of a shallow lake, 30 kilometers (19 miles) from Edmonton. It has a large treed area set aside for those not requiring hookups, but the emphasis is mainly on activities such as fishing, swimming, canoeing, boating, and horseback riding. To get there from downtown, head east on 82nd Avenue to Highway 21, three kilometers (1.9 miles) east of Sherwood Park, then south to Highway 520, then 10 kilometers (6.2 miles) east.

EDMONTON

Food

Eating out in Edmonton used to be identified with the aroma of good ol' Alberta beef wafting from the city's many restaurants, but things are changing. Today, 2,000 restaurants offer a balance of international cuisine and local favorites in all price brackets. From the legendary home-style cooking of Barb and Ernie's to the historic elegance of Madison's Grill, there's something to suit everyone's taste and budget. Restaurants are concentrated in a few main areas. Downtown in the plazas are food courts that fill with office workers, shoppers, and tourists each lunchtime. This part of the city also has some of Edmonton's finest dining establishments. Old Strathcona offers a smorgasbord of choices, with cuisine from all corners of the world. Gateway Boulevard and Calgary Trail, northbound and southbound, respectively, along Highway 2 south of downtown, are lined with family restaurants, buffets, and fast-food outlets.

DOWNTOWN
Cafés and Cheap Eats
Looking north to City Hall, **Three Bananas** (9918 102nd Ave., 780/428-2200, 8 A.M.–7 P.M. Mon.–Fri., 10 A.M.–7 P.M. Sat., 11 A.M.–5 P.M. Sun., lunches $4.50–12) is a bright, inspiring space in the heart of downtown. The menu features the usual array of coffee concoctions, single-serving pizzas, and grilled panini, all made to order. Wireless Internet access is free.

Zenari's (10180 101st St., 780/423-5409, 7 A.M.–6:30 P.M. Mon.–Fri., 8 A.M.–6 P.M. Sat., $5–8) in ManuLife Plaza East is a popular lunchtime deli hangout known for its variety of sandwiches and freshly prepared soups, as well as coffees from around the world, ground fresh to order.

In an inconspicuous spot on the west side of downtown, **Blue Plate Diner** (10145 104th St., 780/429-0740, 11 A.M.–10 P.M. Mon.–Fri., 9 A.M.–10 P.M. Sat.–Sun., $12–18) is a welcoming place, with simple furnishings and a thoughtful menu with dishes made fresh each

day. Vegetarian choices include a delicious lentil and nut loaf doused with miso gravy, while other choices include gourmet mac and cheese and a shrimp stir-fry.

Pub Dining
Surrounded by the city's highest high-rises is the **Sherlock Holmes** (10012 101A Ave., 780/426-7784, from 11:30 A.M. Mon.–Sat., $12–16), a charming English-style pub with a shingled roof, whitewashed walls with black trim, and a white picket fence surrounding it. At lunchtime, it is packed with the office crowd. Try traditional British dishes such as bangers and mash, meat loaf, and steak and mushroom pie washed down with a pint of Newcastle ale or Guinness stout. Still hungry? The bread and butter pudding ($8) is a delicious way to end your meal.

In the West End, the **Sidetrack Cafe** (10238 104th St., 780/421-1326, from 7 A.M. Mon.–Fri., from 9 A.M. weekends, $9–14) has been a music hot spot for over two decades, but it also has a reputation for excellent food. Big, hearty breakfasts cost $4–7.50. Soups, salads, burgers, sandwiches, pizza, and world fare are all on the menu. The soup-and-sandwich lunch deal includes a bottomless bowl of soup. Dinners, served 5–10 P.M., are mostly pub staples.

Canadian
The area along 97th Street has always been Edmonton's own little skid row, but this is changing. Now, it's home to the **(Hardware Grill** (9698 Jasper Ave., 780/423-0969, 11:30 A.M.–1:30 P.M. Mon.–Fri. and from 5 P.M. Mon.–Sat., $30–49), one of the city's finest restaurants. Located at the street level of an early-1900s redbrick building (once a hardware store), the white linen and silver table settings contrast starkly with the restored interior. The menu features dishes using a wide variety of seasonal Canadian produce, including pork, lamb, beef, venison, and salmon, all well prepared and delightfully presented.

At ◖ **Madison's Grill** (Union Bank Inn, 10053 Jasper Ave., 780/401-2222, breakfast and dinner daily, lunch only weekdays, $28–40), the official-looking architecture of this former bank remains, with contemporary styling balancing columns and ornate ceiling. The kitchen features the best in Canadian ingredients, with the Alaskan king crab lasagna a real treat. The lunchtime pan-seared calamari salad keeps up the seafood theme. Good food coupled with impeccable service makes Madison's the perfect place for a splurge.

Although the location at the base of an apartment building is unassuming, the **Copper Pot** (9707 110th St., 780/452-7800, 11 A.M.–10 P.M. Tues.–Fri., 4–10 P.M. Sat., $27–38) is well worth searching out. It's across 109th Street from the legislature building, making it a great lunchtime diversion from seeing the sights of downtown. Seating is tiered, so no one misses out on the views across to the High Level Bridge and beyond, and the setting is bright and modern. At lunch, choose a soup-and-salad combination ($8) or a turkey and Brie clubhouse sandwich ($14). The dinner menu features lots of game and produce sourced from western Canada; bison from the prairies and trout from Great Slave Lake are tasty examples. Diners park for free in the underground lot accessed from 110th Street.

The city's hotels provide further dining options. In general, revolving restaurants are renowned for bad food as much as great views. But **La Ronde** (10111 Bellamy Hill, 780/420-8366, 5:30–10:30 P.M. daily, 10:30 A.M.–2 P.M. Sun. for brunch, $28–39), atop the Crowne Plaza Chateau Lacombe, is an exception. The Canadian-inspired menu features delicacies such as maple-glazed Arctic char, grilled bison rib eye, and east coast lobster, or enjoy a three-course table d'hôte for a reasonable $53.

The **Harvest Room** (Fairmont Hotel Macdonald, 10065 100th St., 780/429-6424, breakfast, lunch, and dinner daily, $28–45) has the look of a cruise-ship dining room of yesteryear but remains remarkably unstuffy. The food itself blends Canadian specialties, sourced locally where possible, with European influences and a very comprehensive wine list. Royal (high) Tea is served each summer afternoon at 3 P.M. (reservations recommended); $33 per person includes a hotel tour.

Asian Fusion

Wild Tangerine (10383 112th St., 780/429-3131, 11:30 A.M.–10 P.M. Mon.–Fri., 5–11:30 P.M. Sat., $13–26) boasts imaginative cooking in a casual, color-filled room. Many dishes have their origins in Asia but have been given a modern makeover with local produce as a base (think grilled salmon dusted with lemon tea or mussels boiled open in red curry). Save room for the chocolate brownie covered in orange marmalade and cream cheese.

European

Among the dozens of Italian restaurants in the city, one of the most popular is **Sorrentino's** (780/424-7500, 11:30 A.M.–10 P.M. Mon.–Fri., 5–10 P.M. Sat., $15–31), with five city locations including downtown at 10162 100th Street. The decor at all locations is stylish, with a great old-world Italian charm. The food is simple and satisfying. Begin with prawns sautéed in a Gorgonzola cream reduction, then move on to a traditionally rich pasta dish, or something lighter such as Greek-style lamb medallions.

As you descend the stairs to **The Creperie** below the Boardwalk Market (10220 103rd St., 780/420-6656, lunch Tues.–Fri., dinner daily, $20–26), a great smell, wafting from somewhere in the depths of this historic building, hits you in the face. It takes a minute for your eyes to adjust to the softly lit dining area, but once you do, its inviting French provincial atmosphere is apparent. As you've probably guessed, crepes are the specialty. Choose from fillings as varied as the Canadian-influenced Crepe Pacific ($20), filled with shrimp, salmon, and asparagus, to the classic chocolate crepe ($8) for dessert.

Cafe Select (10018 106th St., 780/428-1629, 11 A.M.–2 A.M. Mon.–Fri., 5 P.M.–2 A.M. Sat.–Sun., $15–28), nestled below a parking garage just off Jasper Avenue, gives the first impression of being an upscale European-style bistro, and to a degree it is. The restaurant is elegant, soft music is played, and a bunch of intellectuals sip wine and eat oysters until two in the morning. But the food is well priced, and no one seems to mind if you stick to just coffee and dessert. Try the chocolate torte ($8.50).

East Indian

My favorite East Indian restaurant in Edmonton is **Haweli** (10220 103rd St., 780/421-8100, lunch and dinner daily, $14–22), which has an enchantingly simple ambience, complete with silk curtains separating some tables and soothing background music. The food is traditional all the way, with the same menu at lunch and dinner, but mains are mostly under $20.

OLD STRATHCONA AND VICINITY

This historic suburb south of downtown offers Edmonton's largest concentration of cafés and restaurants. There's a great variety of choices, and because it's a popular late-night hangout, many eateries are open to the wee hours.

Coffeehouses

Block 1912 (10361 82nd Ave., 780/433-6575, 9 A.M.–10 P.M. Mon.–Sat., 10 A.M.–10 P.M. Sun.) offers a great variety of hot drinks, cakes, pastries, and healthy full meals in an inviting atmosphere, which includes several comfortable lounges. Newspapers from around the world are available. Brightly lit **Muddy Waters** (8211 111th St., 780/433-4390, 10:30 A.M.–midnight Mon.–Fri., noon–1 A.M. Sat., 4–11 P.M. Sun.) is a popular hangout with students from the nearby university who really know their coffee and like to study into the night.

Mexican and Cajun

Julio's Barrio Mexican Restaurant (10450 Whyte Ave., 780/431-0774, lunch and dinner until midnight daily, $11–19), a huge restaurant decorated with earthy colors and Southwestern-style furniture, has a true Mexican ambience. The menu is appealing but limited. If you just want a light snack, try the warm corn chips with Jack cheese and freshly made salsa ($7.25);

for something more substantial, consider the fajitas, presented in a cast-iron pan. This place doesn't get really busy until after 9 P.M.

Da-de-o (10548 Whyte Ave., 780/433-0930, 11:30 A.M.–11 P.M. Mon.–Tues. and Thurs.–Sat., noon–10 P.M. Sun., $9–18) is styled on a 1950s diner in New Orleans. The menu features Cajun cuisine, including po' boys—Southern-style sandwiches using French bread and fillings such as blackened catfish and tequila salsa ($11)—as well as catfish salad, Southern fried chicken, jambalaya, and inexpensive dishes like barbecue beans and rice that have appeal to the money-watching college crowd. When the hip evening crowd arrives, service can be blasé at best.

Chinese

West of Old Strathcona, toward the University of Alberta, is **Mandarin Restaurant** (11044 82nd Ave., 780/433-8494, 11:30 A.M.–2:30 P.M. Mon.–Fri and from 4:30 P.M. for dinner daily, $9–18), consistently voted as having the best Chinese food in the city, but you'd never know by looking at it. It's informal, noisy, family-style dining, and the walls are plastered with sporting memorabilia donated by diners. Most dishes are from northern China, which is known for traditionally hot food, but enough Cantonese dishes are offered to please all tastes.

Fine Dining

Located a few blocks east of the railway tracks, in a renovated shop, is one of Edmonton's most popular restaurants, the **Unheardof** (9602 82nd Ave., 780/432-0480, from 5:30 P.M. Tues.–Sun., $35–45). The main dining room is filled with antiques, and the tables are set with starched white linen and silver cutlery. The menu changes weekly, featuring fresh game such as venison tenderloin, homemade chutneys, and relishes during fall, and chicken and beef dishes the rest of the year. Desserts such as fruit strudel ($12) top off your meal. Although it's most obviously an upscale restaurant, the service is comfortable, but most importantly, the food is absolutely mouthwatering. Reservations are essential.

A Local Legend

once is enough - huge portions

It feels uncomfortable placing this restaurant straight after the renowned Unheardof, especially since it's not even in Old Strathcona (it's a five-minute drive east, then south), but **Barb and Ernie's** (9906 72nd Ave., 780/433-3242, 7 A.M.–8 P.M. Tues.–Fri., 8 A.M.–8 P.M. Sat., 8 A.M.–3 P.M. Sun., $8–16) needs to be included somewhere, and it doesn't fit anywhere else. Believe it or not, even here in the cultural capital of Canada getting a table at this restaurant, sandwiched between auto-body shops, nearly always entails a wait. Expect vinyl seats, silver chrome chairs, and photos of the owner with his hockey heroes. The home-style cooking is hearty and reasonably priced. Breakfast is busiest, with all the usual for under $10. The rest of the day, hamburgers begin at $8, and German specialties, such as Wiener schnitzel, range $13–16.

Information and Services

Information Centers

For pretrip planning, contact the **Edmonton Economic Development Corporation** (800/463-4667, www.edmonton.com).

The most central source of tourist information is at street level at 9990 Jasper Avenue (opposite the Fairmont Hotel Macdonald, 7 A.M.–7 P.M. Mon.–Fri.). If you're driving up to Edmonton from the south along Highway 2, move over to the right lane as you enter the city in preparation for a stop at the **Gateway Park Visitor Information Centre** (780/496-8400, 8:30 A.M.–4:30 P.M. Mon.–Fri., 9 A.M.–5 P.M. Sat.–Sun.). Within this complex, you'll find interpretive displays on the oil industry, stands filled with brochures, and direct-dial phones for Edmonton accommodations. On the Arrivals level of the **Edmonton International Airport** is an information booth (8 A.M.–midnight Mon.–Fri. and 9 A.M.–midnight Sat.–Sun. year-round).

© ANDREW HEMPSTEAD

Approaching from the south, Gateway Park Visitor Information Centre should be your first stop.

An excellent source of information on Alberta's provincial parks, forest reserves, and other protected areas is the **Alberta Environment Information Centre** (9820 106th St., 780/427-2700, www.environment.alberta.ca, 8:15 A.M.–4:30 P.M. Mon.–Fri.).

Libraries

Edmonton Public Library (www.epl.ca) has 16 branches spread throughout the city. The largest is the **Stanley A. Milner Library** (7 Sir Winston Churchill Square, 780/496-7000, 9 A.M.–9 P.M. Mon.–Fri., 9 A.M.–6 P.M. Sat., 1–5 P.M. Sun.). This large, two-story facility, connected to the downtown core by pedways, is a great place to spend a rainy afternoon. It carries newspapers, magazines, and phone books from all corners of the globe, as well as rows and rows of western Canadiana. Throughout the week, author readings take place on the main level.

Post and Internet

The main **post office** is downtown at 9808 103A Avenue (780/944-3273).

All downtown hotels have in-room Internet access, while most others have Wi-Fi or an Internet booth in the lobby. Public Internet access is free at all city libraries, or you can pay approximately $5 for 30 minutes downtown at the **Bohemia Cyber Café** (11812 Jasper Ave., 780/429-3442, 10 A.M.–1 A.M. Mon.–Fri., 11 A.M.–1 A.M. Sat., 11 A.M.–midnight Sun.).

Banks

Main branches of most banks in the downtown area will handle common foreign-currency exchange transactions, as will **Calforex** (780/484-3868), at the entrance nearest to Galaxyland in West Edmonton Mall. Edmonton International Airport has a foreign exchange on the departures level.

Laundry

On the west side of the city is **LaPerle Home-style Laundry** (9756 182nd St., 780/483-9200), which is handy to the hotels in the area and has large washers and dryers for sleeping bags. **The Laundry** (10808 107th Ave., 780/424-8981) is closer to downtown. The **Soap Time Laundromat** (7626 104th St., 780/439-3599) is open until 11:30 P.M.

Emergency Services

For medical emergencies, call 911 or one of the following hospitals: **Grey Nuns Community Hospital** (corner of 34th Ave. and 66th St., 780/735-7000), **Northeast Community Health Centre** (14007 50th St., 780/472-5000), **Royal Alexandra Hospital** (10240 Kingsway Ave., 780/735-4111), or **University of Alberta Hospital** (8440 112th St., 780/407-8822). For the **Edmonton Police Service,** call 780/423-4567.

Getting There and Around

GETTING THERE

Air

Edmonton International Airport (YEG, www.flyeia.com) is beside Highway 2, 29 kilometers (18 miles) south of the city center. Canada's fifth-largest airport, it has undergone a transformation over the last decade, with construction slated to continue until 2012, paid for in part by the Airport Improvement Fee ($15) built into all tickets for departing flights. On the Arrivals level is a small information booth (8 A.M.–midnight Mon.–Fri. and 9 A.M.–midnight Sat.–Sun. year-round). Also at the airport are car-rental desks, hotel courtesy phones, a restaurant, and a currency exchange. **Sky Shuttle** (780/465-8515 or 888/438-2342, www.edmontonskyshuttle.com) departs the airport for downtown hotels every 20 minutes (every 30 minutes on weekends) on three different routes. One-way to downtown is $15, round-trip $30; check in at the counter beside the information center. The cab fare to downtown is around $50 one-way.

Parking is $3.25 for 30 minutes to a maximum of $22 for any 24-hour period. Long-term parking is available at other places nearby as well. For a regular-size car, **Value Park** (780/890-8439) charges $13 per day or $65 for a full week.

Rail

The **VIA Rail station** is a small, modern building beyond the west end of the City Centre Airport northwest of downtown (12360 121st St., 800/561-8630, www.viarail.ca). The ticket office is generally open 8 A.M.–3:30 P.M. daily, later when trains are due. A Hertz rental outlet is also open for arriving and departing trains, but reservations are necessary. Trains leave Vancouver (1150 Station Street) and Prince Rupert three times weekly for the 23.5-hour trip to Edmonton (via Jasper), continuing on the Canadian route to the eastern provinces.

Bus

The **Greyhound** bus depot (10324 103rd St., 780/420-2400 or 800/661-8747, www.greyhound.ca, 5:30 A.M.–midnight Mon.–Sat., 10 A.M.–6 P.M. Sun.) is within walking distance of the city center and many hotels. Within the depot is an A&W Restaurant, a small paper shop, a cash machine, and large lockers ($2). Buses leave daily for all points in Canada, including Calgary (3.5 hours), Jasper (4.5 hours), and Vancouver (15–17 hours). As always with Greyhound, no seat assignments are given—just turn up, buy your ticket, and hop aboard. You can also buy discounted tickets seven days in advance. If you plan to travel extensively by bus, the Discovery Pass is a good deal.

Red Arrow (780/424-3339, www.redarrow.ca) buses leave Edmonton five to seven times daily for Red Deer and Calgary and once daily for Fort McMurray. The downtown office and pickup point is off to one side of the Holiday Inn Express (10014 104th St.).

GETTING AROUND

Reaching Edmonton's most popular attractions is easy using public transit, but the road system and clear signage makes driving relatively simple also. Major highways from the east, west, and south converge on downtown, with bypasses such as Whitemud Drive (for those traveling from the south to West Edmonton Mall) making avoiding downtown easy.

Bus

The **Edmonton Transit System** (780/496-1611, www.edmonton.ca) operates an extensive bus system that links the city center to all parts of the city and many major sights. Not all routes operate on Sunday. For many destinations south of the North Saskatchewan River, you'll need to jump aboard the Light Rail Transit (LRT) to the University Transfer Point. Bus fare anywhere within the city is $2.50 per person; transfers are available on boarding and can be used for additional travel in any direction within 90 minutes. Day passes are $7.50. For more information and passes, go to the Customer Services Outlet at the Churchill LRT Station on 99th Street (780/496-1622, 8:30 A.M.–4:30 P.M. weekdays).

Light Rail Transit

The LRT has 15 stops (Canada's smallest subway system) running east–west along Jasper Avenue (101st Avenue), northeast as far as Whitemud Park, and south to Century Park, with a northeast extension slated for completion in 2014. The LRT runs underground through the city center, connecting with many pedways. Travel between Grandin and Churchill is free 9 A.M.–3 P.M. Monday–Friday and 9 A.M.–6 P.M. Saturday. LRT tickets are the same price as the bus, and tickets, transfers, and day passes are valid for travel on either the LRT or the bus system.

High Level Street Car

A great way to travel between downtown and Old Strathcona is on the High Level Street Car (780/437-7721, $3 one-way). Trains and trams originally traveled this historic route over the High Level Bridge, but today a restored streetcar makes the journey from the west side of the Alberta Legislature Building to Old Strathcona between mid-May and August every 30 minutes 11 A.M.–4 P.M. Sunday–Friday and 9 A.M.–4 P.M. Saturday. Round-trip fare is $4.

Passengers with Disabilities

Edmonton Transit operates the Disabled Adult Transit System (DATS, 780/496-4567), which provides access to various points of the city for passengers with physical disabilities who are unable to use the regular transit system. The door-to-door service costs the same as Edmonton Transit adult tickets. Priority is given to those heading to work or for medical trips. A Pedway Information Sheet, detailing accessibility, is available from City Hall (780/424-4085).

Taxis

The standard flag charge for cabs is $3.29 plus approximately $1.85 per kilometer, but most companies have flat rates for major destinations within the city. Major companies are **Alberta Co-op Taxi Line** (780/425-2525), **Checker Cabs** (780/484-8888), **Prestige Cabs** (780/462-4444), and **Yellow Cab** (780/462-3456).

Car Rental

If you've just arrived in Edmonton, call around and compare rates. All major agencies include unlimited mileage and built-in charges for airport pickups. They also provide free pickup and drop-off at major Edmonton hotels and have outlets at the airport. Rental agencies and their local numbers are **Avis** (780/448-0066), **Budget** (780/448-2000), **Discount** (780/448-3888), **Enterprise** (780/440-4550), **Hertz** (780/415-5283), **National** (780/422-6097), **Rent-a-Wreck** (780/986-3335), and **Thrifty** (780/890-4555).

NORTHERN ALBERTA

The northern half of Alberta, from Highway 16 north to the 60th parallel, is a sparsely populated land of unspoiled wilderness, home to deer, moose, coyote, fox, lynx, black bear, and the elusive Swan Hills grizzly bear. For the most part, it is heavily forested, part of the boreal forest ecoregion that sweeps around the Northern Hemisphere, broken only by the Atlantic and Pacific Oceans. Much of the world's boreal forest has been devastated by logging, but in northern Alberta a good portion of the land is muskeg—low-lying bogs and marshes that make logging difficult and expensive. Only a few species of trees are adapted to the long, cold winters and short summer growing seasons characteristic of these northern latitudes. Conifers such as white spruce, black spruce, jack pine, fir, and larch are the most common.

This vast expanse of land is relatively flat, the only exceptions being the Swan Hills—which rise to 1,200 meters (3,900 feet)—and, farther north, the Birch and Caribou Mountains. The Athabasca and Peace River Systems are the region's largest waterways. Carrying water from hundreds of tributaries, they merge in the far northeastern corner of the province and flow north into the Arctic Ocean. A third major watercourse, the North Saskatchewan River, flows east from the Continental Divide, crossing northern Alberta on its way to Hudson Bay. Alberta's earliest explorers arrived along these rivers, opening up the Canadian West to the trappers, missionaries, and settlers who followed.

Northeast of Edmonton is the Lakeland region, where many early fur-trading posts were

© ANDREW HEMPSTEAD

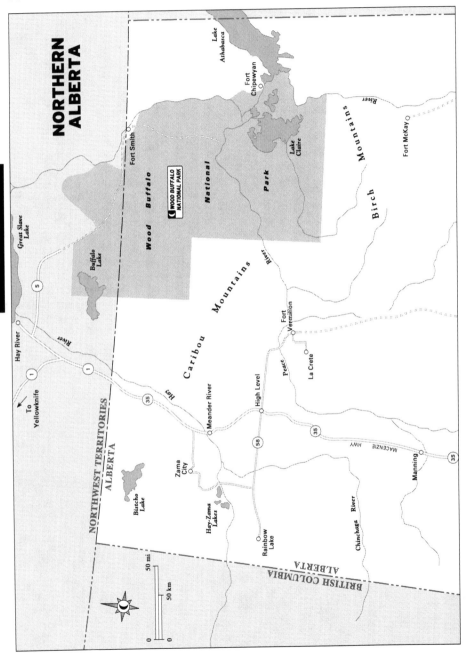

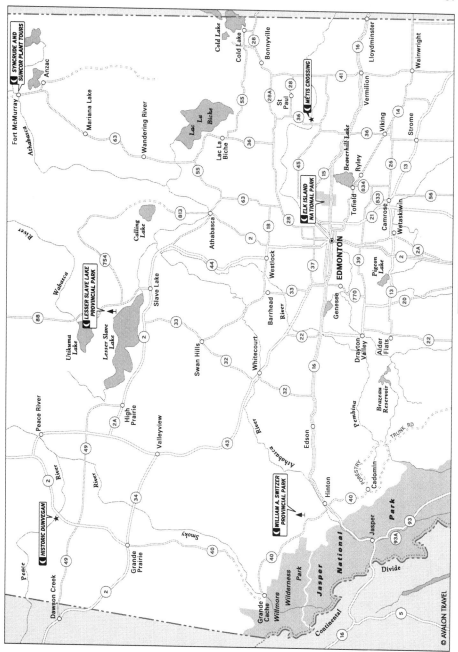

NORTHERN ALBERTA

© AVALON TRAVEL

NORTHERN ALBERTA

HIGHLIGHTS

◖ **Elk Island National Park:** Nowhere else in the province has the wildlife-viewing opportunities of this small park. Sightings of elk, moose, and bison are (almost) guaranteed (page 54).

◖ **Métis Crossing:** This, Canada's largest Métis cultural center, spreads across a river-front site important for its historical links to native peoples and fur traders (page 61).

◖ **Syncrude and Suncor Plant Tours:** As Fort McMurray has more oil reserves than the rest of the world combined, it's no surprise that it is booming. The best way to take it all in is on one of these bus tours (page 72).

◖ **Wood Buffalo National Park:** A visit to the world's second-largest national park requires time and money, but visitors will be rewarded with the sight of the world's largest free-roaming herd of bison (page 78).

◖ **Lesser Slave Lake Provincial Park:** Alberta isn't renowned for its white sandy beaches and beautiful over-water sunsets, but this large park has both (page 85).

◖ **William A. Switzer Provincial Park:** Dotted with fish-filled lakes and home to abundant big game, this park is a great place for outdoor enthusiasts to pitch a tent for a night or two (page 97).

◖ **Historic Dunvegan:** Dating to 1885, the missionary buildings at this site are in beautiful condition. And if you're not a history buff, there's a colorful suspension bridge to admire (page 107).

LOOK FOR ◖ TO FIND RECOMMENDED SIGHTS, ACTIVITIES, DINING, AND LODGING.

established. From there, Highway 63 heads north through boreal forest to Fort McMurray, an isolated city of 48,000, 450 kilometers (280 miles) north of its closest sizable neighbor, Edmonton. Oil is Fort McMurray's raison d'être—oil sands, to be precise. The Athabasca Oil Sands are the world's largest such deposit, and the city is booming.

North-central Alberta extends from Edmonton's outer suburbs north to the towns of Athabasca and Slave Lake, which are jumping-off points into the vast boreal forest. This area is a paradise for bird-watchers because it's at the confluence of three major flyways.

West of Edmonton, the Yellowhead Highway climbs into the Canadian Rockies, passing through Hinton, a town surrounded by natural wonders. From Hinton, travelers can continue on Highway 16 into Jasper National Park, or take Highway 40 northwest to Willmore Wilderness Park, a park usually ignored by tourists in favor of the neighboring national parks to the south. Continuing north on Highway 4, you come to Grande Prairie, one of northern Alberta's largest cities and a regional agriculture and service center. The Peace River Valley, north of Grande Prairie, leads travelers into the Northwest Territories via the Mackenzie Highway (Highway 35), which parallels the Peace and Hay Rivers.

With few regular "sights," northern Alberta receives fewer tourists than the rest of the province. Those who do venture north find solitude in a vast untapped wilderness with abundant wildlife and plenty of recreation—lakes and rivers to fish, historic sites to explore, rivers to float on, and gravel roads to drive just for the sake of it.

PLANNING YOUR TIME

The region covered in this chapter is similar in size to all the other chapters combined and is relatively remote. One week in Alberta just isn't enough time to include this region, but with two weeks and a special interest (such as fishing or camping), you should plan on including at least a portion of the region in your itinerary. The exception to this is **Elk Island National Park,** close enough to Edmonton to make it part of a trip to that city. On a two- or three-day loop from the capital, you could include this park, plus cultural Lakeland highlights such as **Métis Crossing** while returning via the sandy beaches of **Lesser Slave Lake Provincial Park.** Fort McMurray is the center of world attention for its oil sands, and although it's a long drive (or a short flight), a visit could be compared to spending time in a boomtown of a century ago, like Dawson City. But don't trek north without reservations for accommodation and a **Syncrude/Suncor plant tour.** If you dedicate a full week to northern Alberta, plan on hitting the highlights already mentioned, and then heading west through Hinton to **William A. Switzer Provincial Park,** with its abundant wildlife and great fishing, and north to the Peace Country, where places like **Historic Dunvegan** have changed little since the days of the missionaries. The wilderness of **Wood Buffalo National Park,** in the northeast corner of the province, is only accessible by road through the Northwest Territories, making it a natural extension of a visit to that province. But those with a sense of adventure can fly north from Fort McMurray to Fort Chipewyan and reach the park by boat.

Lakeland

Highway 16, east from Edmonton, follows the southern flanks of a region containing hundreds of lakes formed at the end of the last ice age by a retreating sheet of ice nearly one kilometer (0.6 mile) thick. From its headwaters beneath the Columbia Icefield on the Continental Divide, the **North Saskatchewan River** flows east through Edmonton and the Lakeland region before eventually draining into Hudson Bay.

History buffs appreciate the legacies of early white settlers that dot the landscape here—restored fur-trading posts, missions, and the Ukrainian Village near Vegreville. Other visitors are attracted by the region's vast areas of unspoiled wilderness, including seven provincial parks. Anglers will feel right at home among the area's countless lakes, and wildlife-watchers are drawn to Elk Island National Park, which rivals Tanzania's Serengeti Plain for the population densities of its animal inhabitants.

The region's major population centers are Lloydminster (250 km/155 miles east of Edmonton), Canada's only town in two provinces; St. Paul, which has the world's only

NORTHERN ALBERTA

© AVALON TRAVEL

UFO landing pad; and Cold Lake, at the edge of the boreal forest, surrounded by vast reserves of untapped oil.

◖ ELK ISLAND NATIONAL PARK

Heading east from Edmonton on Highway 16, you'll reach Elk Island National Park in well under an hour. This small, fenced, 194-square-kilometer (75-square-mile) park preserves a remnant of the transitional grassland ecoregion—the aspen parkland—that once covered the entire northern flank of the prairie. It's also one of the best spots in Alberta for wildlife-watching; with approximately 3,000 large mammals, the park has one of the highest concentrations of big game in the world.

The park was originally set aside in 1906 to protect a herd of elk; it's Canada's only national park formed to protect a native species. The elk here have never been crossbred and are probably the most genetically pure in the world. In addition to approximately 1,600 elk, resident mammals include moose, two species of bison, white-tailed and mule deer, coyote, beaver, muskrat, mink, and porcupine. The many lakes and wetland areas in the park serve as nesting sites for waterfowl, and approximately 230 species of birds have been observed here.

A mosaic of mixed-wood forest—predominantly aspen and balsam poplar—covers the low, rolling Beaver Hills, slowly taking over the grassland. One slow-moving stream winds its way through the park, and many shallow lakes dot the landscape.

Park entry for one day is adult $7.90, senior $6.90, child $3.90 to a maximum of $20 per vehicle; if you've purchased an annual pass, you'll be waved straight through the fee station (but stop to pick up park information anyway).

Bison in the Park

Two different species of bison inhabit the park, and to prevent interbreeding, they are separated. All bison on the north side of Highway 16 are **plains bison,** whereas those on the south side are **wood bison.**

Before the late 1700s, 60 million plains bison lived on the North American plains. In less than a century, humanity brought these shaggy beasts to the brink of extinction. By 1880, incredibly, only a few hundred plains bison remained. A small herd, owned by ranchers in Montana, was brought north in 1907. They were held at what was then Elk Island Reserve until Buffalo National Park (since closed) at Wainwright was fenced. When it came time to move the animals from Elk Island, some couldn't be found, and today's herd descended from those well-hidden progenitors. A small part of the herd is kept in a large enclosure just north of the Park Information Centre, whereas others roam freely through the north section of the park. Today they number approximately 630 within the park.

The wood bison, the largest native land mammal in North America, was thought to be extinct for many years—a victim of hunting, severe winters, and interbreeding with its close relative, the plains bison. In 1957, a herd of 200 was discovered in the remote northwestern corner of Wood Buffalo National Park. Some were captured and transported to the Mackenzie Bison Sanctuary in the Northwest Territories and to Elk Island National Park. The herd at Elk Island has ensured the survival of the species, and today it is the purest herd in the world. It is used as breeding stock for several captive herds throughout North America. To view the herd of 400, look south

ELK ISLAND NATIONAL PARK

© AVALON TRAVEL

NORTHERN ALBERTA

© ANDREW HEMPSTEAD

Elk Island National Park is best known for its bison.

from Highway 16 or hike the Wood Bison Trail.

Hiking

Twelve trails, ranging 1.4–18.5 kilometers (0.9–11.5 miles) in length, cover all areas of the park and provide excellent opportunities to view wildlife. A park information sheet details each one. Make sure to carry water with you, though, because surface water in the park is not suitable for drinking. The paved **Shoreline Trail** (3 km/1.9 miles one-way) follows the shore of Astotin Lake from the golf course parking lot. The **Lakeview Trail** (3.3 km/two miles round-trip) begins from the northern end of the recreation area and provides good views of the lake. Hike this trail in the evening for a chance to see beavers. The only trail on the south side of Highway 16 is the **Wood Bison Trail** (18.6 km/11.5 miles round-trip), which has an interpretive display at the trailhead. In winter, the trails provide excellent cross-country skiing and snowshoeing.

Other Recreation

The day-use area at **Astotin Lake,** 14 kilometers (8.7 miles) north of Highway 16, is the center of much activity. There's a pleasant beach and picnic area; canoes, rowboats, and small sailboats can be rented; and the rolling fairways of adjacent **Elk Island Golf Course** (780/998-3161, weekdays $32, weekends $36) provide an interesting diversion for golfers.

Accommodations and Camping

Sandy Beach Campground, on the north side of the Astotin Lake day-use area, is the only overnight facility within the park. It has fire pits, picnic tables, flush toilets, and showers; $26 per night, plus $9 for a firewood permit. If you're traveling in the peak of summer (especially on weekends), it is strongly recommended to use the **Parks Canada Campground Reservation Service** (905/426-4648 or 877/737-3783, www.pccamping.ca, nonrefundable $11 reservation fee). The main campground is only open in summer; the rest of the year, primitive camping (no water, chemical toilets) is available at

© ANDREW HEMPSTEAD

Astotin Lake, Elk Island National Park

NORTHERN ALBERTA

the boat-launch area. A concession selling fast food and basic camping supplies operates May–October at Astotin Lake, and the golf course (780/998-3161) has a casual restaurant.

If the weather isn't cooperating, there's an alternative to camping—continue north through the park to the hamlet of Lamont, where **Archie's Motel** (5008 49th Ave., 780/895-2225; $50 s, $65 d) has a few basic rooms.

Information
The **Park Information Centre** (780/992-5790, 10 A.M.–6 P.M. Sat.–Sun.May–June, 10 A.M.–6 P.M. daily July–Aug.) is less than one kilometer (0.6 mile) north of Highway 16 on the Elk Island Parkway. For online information, click through the links on the Parks Canada website (www.pc.gc.ca).

EAST ALONG THE YELLOWHEAD HIGHWAY
Blackfoot Recreation Area
South of Elk Island National Park is the 97-square-kilometer (34-square-mile) Cooking

Lake–Blackfoot Recreation Area. It is an integrated resource management unit, meaning that it can be used for many purposes, including grazing, mineral exploration, hunting, and recreation. It is part of the massive Cooking Lake Moraine, formed during the last ice age as the retreating sheet of ice stalled for a time, leaving mounds and hollows that have since filled with water. Large natural areas of wetland and forest provide habitat for abundant wildlife, including moose, elk, white-tailed deer, coyote, beaver, and more than 200 species of birds. Much of the well-posted trail system is for hikers only, but some parts are open to horses and mountain bikes. The **Blackfoot Staging Area,** off Highway 16, is the trailhead for a good selection of short hiking trails, but to really get into the heart of the area, head south along the southwestern border of Elk Island National Park to three other staging areas.

Ukrainian Cultural Heritage Village
This heritage village (50 km/31 miles east of Edmonton, 780/662-3640, 10 A.M.–6 P.M. daily

Lakeland wetlands

late May–Aug., 10 A.M.–6 P.M. Sat.–Sun. Sept., adult $8, senior $7, child $4) is a realistic replica of a Ukrainian settlement, common in the rural areas of east-central Alberta at the turn of the 20th century. The first, and largest, Ukrainian settlement in Canada was located in this region. Driven from their homeland in Eastern Europe, Ukrainians fled to the Canadian prairies where, for many years, they dressed and worked in the ways of the Old World. These traditions are kept alive with costumed guides and a lively program of cultural events.

Vegreville

Although first settled by French farmers from Kansas, this town of 5,300 is best known for its Ukrainian heritage. Today Vegreville's biggest attraction is the world's largest *pysanka*, a giant, traditionally decorated Ukrainian Easter egg at the east end of town. It measures eight meters (26 feet) in length, weighs 2,270 kilograms (5,000 pounds), and can turn in the wind like a giant weathervane.

Vegreville celebrates its multicultural past on Canada Day (July 1) weekend with the **Ukrainian Pysanka Folk Festival.**

Vermilion

The reddish-colored iron deposits in a nearby river gave this town of 4,300 at the junction of Highways 16 and 41 its name. Many downtown buildings date to the 1919–1920 period after a fire destroyed the original main street (50th Avenue) in 1918. Made of locally fired brick, many have plaques detailing their history. Pick up a walking-tour brochure at the information center (10 A.M.–6 P.M. daily in summer) by the entrance to town. In an impressive 1928 school building, **Vermilion Heritage Museum** (50th Ave. at 53rd St., 780/853-6211, 1–5 P.M. daily mid-June–Aug., donation) holds an extensive photographic collection and native artifacts.

Vermilion Provincial Park is one of only two urban-area provincial parks in Alberta. The park encompasses 771 hectares (1,900 acres) of aspen parkland and grassland along the banks of the Vermilion River, an ancient glacial meltwater channel. To date, 20 species of mammals and 110 species of birds have been documented here. The park also has 15 kilometers (9.3 miles) of hiking trails and a campground with showers and a trout pond ($20–38). Access is from the west side of town, north along 62nd Street. This road winds around the back of a residential area, passes a 1905 Canadian National Railway station (relocated), and then descends to a riverside day-use area.

LLOYDMINSTER

North America has several twin cities that straddle borders (such as Minneapolis and St. Paul), but Lloydminster is the only one that has a single corporate body in two provinces (or states, depending on the case). Approximately 60 percent of the city's 22,000 residents live on the Alberta side, separated from their Saskatchewan neighbors by the main street.

Lloydminster was settled in 1903 by over 1,000 immigrants from Britain, who followed the Reverend George Lloyd to the site in search of good agricultural land. The community thrived, and when the provinces of Alberta and Saskatchewan were created out of the Northwest Territories in 1905, the town was divided by the new border, which ran along

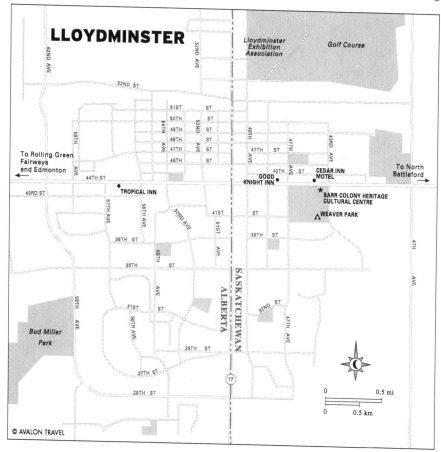

the fourth meridian. It functioned as two separate communities until 1930, when community leaders requested that the two halves be amalgamated into the City of Lloydminster. Farming and cattle ranching form the base of the regional economy, although oil and natural gas play an important role in the city's future.

Sights

The **Barr Colony Heritage Cultural Centre** (4515 44th St., 306/825-5655, 10 A.M.–8 P.M. daily July–Aug., 10 A.M.–5 P.M. Tues.–Sat. the rest of the year, adult $6.75, child $4.75) houses the Richard Larsen Museum, featuring a collection of artifacts and antiques used by early

settlers. Also here, the Imhoff Art Gallery contains more than 200 works of early-1900s artist Count Berthold Von Imhoff, a room is dedicated to describing oil sands technology, and a number of historic buildings dot the courtyard.

The 81-hectare (200-acre) **Bud Miller Park** (south of Hwy. 16 along 59th Ave., 780/875-4497, 7 A.M.–11 P.M. daily) offers several nature trails winding around a two-hectare (five-acre) lake and through stands of aspen. Canada's largest sundial, a tree maze, formal gardens, an arboretum, a nature center, and boat rentals can also be found here.

Accommodations and Food

Although it looks decidedly untropical from the outside, **Tropical Inn** (5621 44th St., 780/825-7000 or 800/219-5244, www.tropicalinns.com, $105–155 s or d) will be a hit with kids for its indoor waterslide and pool complex. The 165 guest rooms are surprisingly appealing, with nice extras such as dry cleaning and high-speed Internet rounding out a good choice for overnight accommodations. A couple of cheapies on the Saskatchewan side of the border are **Cedar Inn Motel** (4526 44th St., 306/825-6155, $58 s, $68 d) and the air-conditioned **Good Knight Inn** (4729 44th St., 306/825-0124, $65 s, $78 d).

Weaver Park Campsite (behind the Barr Colony Centre, 306/825-3726, unserviced sites $15, hookups $20–25) has showers and a grocery store. Much nicer is **Rolling Green Fairways** (780/875-4653, www.lloydminstergolf.com, $28–30), two kilometers (1.2 miles) west of the city on Highway 16, then one kilometer (0.6 mile) north. Facilities include showers, a laundry room, free firewood, and, as the name suggests, an adjacent golf course.

The **Tea House** (south side of Hwy. 16, just east of the border post) was built in 1942 and is surrounded by well-established gardens. Afternoon tea and light lunches are served 10 A.M.–5 P.M. Tuesday–Saturday April–December. Local favorites are the Irish pub and **Tony Roma's** restaurant in the Tropical Inn (5621 44th St., 780/825-7000); the latter is open for breakfast.

LIVING IN LLOYDMINSTER

Living in a town in two provinces can be confusing. Saskatchewan has a 5 percent provincial sales tax, but to make it more equitable for local businesses competing with those in a tax-free province that is literally across the road, the provincial government has exempted them from collecting the tax. The liquor store on the Alberta side is always busier – Alberta's booze is cheaper. The minimum drinking age is 19 in Saskatchewan, but 18-year-olds can just cross the road into Alberta to drink. Natural gas is supplied to all residents by an Alberta company, but only residents on the Alberta side get a government rebate. Albertans pay a monthly fee for health care (Saskatchewan residents get it for free), even though everyone goes to a hospital on the Saskatchewan side. The minimum wage is higher in Saskatchewan and vacations are longer, but income tax is higher. The best strategy might be to live in Alberta and work in Saskatchewan; houses on the Alberta side are up to 30 percent more expensive, but the province has lower taxes, and with a job in Saskatchewan – where the benefits are better – you'd come out in front eventually.

Information

The best source of information once you arrive in town is the provincially operated **Travel Alberta Information Centre** (1 km/0.6 mile east of town, 9 A.M.–5 P.M. daily mid-May–mid-June, 8 A.M.–6 P.M. daily in summer). The **Saskatchewan Visitor Reception Centre** (beside the Barr Colony Centre, 306/825-8690, 9 A.M.–5 P.M. daily in spring, 8 A.M.–6 P.M. daily in summer) also has information on the town but is mainly a source of information for those heading east.

HIGHWAY 28 TO SMOKY LAKE

Highway 28 leaves Edmonton heading north through the suburbs. After a series of 90-degree turns—first one way, then the other, then back again—it comes to **Waskatenau,** where it straightens out to pursue an easterly direction heading toward Cold Lake.

Long Lake Provincial Park

During the last ice age, the low-lying area occupied by this 764-hectare (1,890-acre) park was part of a deep glacial meltwater channel that has now filled with water. Today it's surrounded by boreal forest, although aspens predominate in the park because of fires over the years. Fishing is great here because the main body of water holds some lunker northern pike, as well as perch and walleye. Right on the lake is a 220-site campground (780/576-3959, Apr.–Oct., unserviced sites $20, powered sites $26), with flush toilets, showers, a grocery store, and canoe rentals. To get there from Highway 28, head north from Waskatenau on Highway 831 for 48 kilometers (30 miles).

Immediately to the south of the park is the **White Earth Valley Natural Area,** a 2,055-hectare (5,080-acre) tract of land set aside to protect the habitat of the abundant wildlife and waterfowl.

Smoky Lake

Named for a lake 93 kilometers (58 miles) west of St. Paul, where natives once rested and smoked pipes during hunts, this small town is home to the **Smoky Lake Fair** (www.smoky-lake.com), which revolves around an annual competition to find the largest pumpkin. But don't waste time scanning the vegetable section at your local supermarket for a winner; you'll need a pumpkin weighing at least 340 kilograms (750 pounds) to take the day at Smoky Lake (the world record is 513 kg/1,130 pounds). For those who don't consider size important, there's always a prize for the ugliest pumpkin (officially, only "aesthetically challenged" pumpkins can be entered, appeasing the politically correct) and the pumpkin that's traveled the farthest. Celebrations take place the first weekend of October out at the agricultural complex at the junction of Highways 28 and 855. The official weigh-in takes place on Saturday at noon and is followed by a pig roast and, on Sunday, the Pumpkin Classic Golf Tournament.

VICTORIA TRAIL

Take Highway 855 south from Smoky Lake for 10 kilometers (6.2 miles) to reach Victoria Trail, an unpaved road along the north side of the North Saskatchewan River.

◖ Métis Crossing

At the junction of Highway 855 and Victoria Trail, Métis Crossing (780/656-2229, 11 A.M.–6 P.M. daily mid-May–Aug., adult $5, senior and child $3, family $10) is the country's largest cultural center dedicated to the Métis, the descendants of those born as the result of relationships between French traders and native Cree women. George McDougall established a mission on the site in 1862, and within a decade it was surrounded by a bustling Métis community, who used the riverfront setting as a hub for trade. The restoration project is still in its infancy (the first phase opened in late 2006), but already there are plenty of things to do and see, including a restored barn containing the story of the people's role in the fur trade and how a distinct culture emerged. Also on-site are a craft store, playground, and campground.

Victoria Settlement

Victoria Settlement (7 km/4.3 miles east of

Hwy. 855, 780/656-2333, 10 A.M.–6 P.M. daily mid-May–Aug., adult $3, senior $2, child $1.50) is the perfect complement to Métis Crossing. In 1864, the Hudson's Bay Company established a fur-trading post at the site. The post closed in 1897 and was abandoned until the early 1900s, when groups of Ukrainian settlers moved to the area and the settlement became known as Victoria-Pakan. When the railway bypassed the settlement in 1918, businesses moved north to Smoky Lake, and the area was abandoned once again. Head to the 1906 Methodist church for a slideshow about the settlement or wander past the clerk's 1864 log cabin to the river and the graves of the founder's three daughters. Picnic tables are set among broad maple trees, which were planted during the fur-trading days.

From Victoria Settlement, you can continue south on Highway 855, which eventually intersects Highway 16 west of Vegreville. Along the way, you'll pass by **Andrew,** home of the world's largest mallard duck. Be careful not to rip your jeans climbing the fence to touch it.

ST. PAUL

This town of 5,100, 210 kilometers (130 miles) northeast of Edmonton, has spent many thousands of dollars developing an attraction that hasn't had a single official visitor in over 30 years. And the skeptics doubt it ever will. You guessed it (or maybe you didn't), St. Paul has the world's only **UFO landing pad**—a raised platform beside the main road forlornly waiting for a visitor from outer space. Beside the pad, the **tourist information center** (50th Ave. at 53rd St., 780/645-6800, 8:30 A.M.–4:30 P.M. daily mid-June–mid-Sept.) has interesting displays, including photos of *real* UFOs as well as descriptions of some famous hoaxes. The building is a raised, UFO-shaped circular structure; if approaching from outer space, look for the green flashing light on top.

The town's origins date to 1896, when Father Albert Lacombe, the famed Western missionary, established a settlement where Métis people—who had been largely ignored by the government during treaty talks—could live

and learn farming skills. Lacombe extended an open invitation to all Métis in western Canada, but fewer than 300 responded. After 10 years of hardship, he opened the settlement to whites, attracting people from many cultures. The town's diverse background is cataloged at the **People's Museum Society of St. Paul** (5413 50th Ave., 780/645-5562, 10 A.M.–4 P.M. daily in summer). At the south end of town (head down 47th Street) is **Upper Therien Lake.** More than 200 species of birds have been recorded around this and other nearby lakes. A large stretch of land along Lakeshore Drive has been set aside as a park, with picnic shelters and paths leading out to the lake.

Accommodations

Rooms at the **King's Motel** (5638 50th Ave., 780/645-5656 or 800/265-7407, from $69 s, $79 d) each come with a fridge and microwave. **St. Paul Overnight Trailer Park** (55th St. at 49th Ave., May–Sept., unserviced sites $15, powered sites $20), which has showers, is a short walk from the golf course. **Westcove Municipal Recreation Area** (16 km/10 miles north of St. Paul, 780/645-6688, mid-May–mid-Sept., unserviced sites powered sites $20) is beside a beach on the shore of Vincent Lake and has all facilities.

ST. PAUL TO LLOYDMINSTER

Twenty-eight kilometers (17 miles) east of St. Paul, Highway 28 makes a 90-degree left turn at its junction with Highway 41 and resumes its northeasterly course toward Cold Lake. Those heading back to Highway 16 can turn right at this junction and either beeline directly south on Highway 41 to Vermilion or wind around the backwoods to Lloydminster, taking in the following sights.

Nine kilometers (5.6 miles) south of the Highway 28/41 junction is the hamlet of **Elk Point**—look for a large mural outlining the history of the area along 50th Avenue and an 11-meter (36-foot) statue of explorer Peter Fidler at the north end of town. Turn left (east) onto Highway 646, and soon you'll come to Fort George and the Buckingham House.

Fort George/Buckingham House

The site of these two fur-trading posts on the north bank of the North Saskatchewan River has been designated a Provincial Historical Site (13 km/eight miles east of Elk Point, 780/724-2611, 10 A.M.–6 P.M. daily mid-May–Aug., adult $3, senior $2, child $1.50). In 1792, soon after the North West Company had established Fort George, the Hudson's Bay Company followed suit a few hundred steps away with Buckingham House. Both posts were abandoned in the early 1800s and have long since been destroyed; depressions in the ground, piles of stone, and indistinct pathways are all that remain. Above the site is an interpretive center with audio and visual presentations explaining the rivalry between the two companies and the history of the forts. Interpretive trails lead from the center down to the river.

Lindbergh

Ever wondered where that salt on your dining table came from? Take a tour of the **Canadian Salt Company** (3 km/1.9 miles east of Fort George/Buckingham House, 780/724-3745), owned by the Windsor Salt conglomerate, to find out. A vast reserve of salt left behind when the ocean that once covered Alberta receded lies deep below the earth's surface (1,000 meters/3,300 feet underground) in the vicinity of Lindbergh. It is harvested via a simple yet effective process that pumps water into the bed of salt, creating a brine that is then brought to the surface and boiled to separate the salt from impurities. Hour-long tours of the facility are available 9 A.M.–2 P.M. weekdays (free, reservations necessary).

Whitney Lakes Provincial Park

Whitney, Ross, Laurier, and Borden Lakes are the namesake attractions at this 1,490-hectare (3,680-acre) park on Highway 646. The fishing is excellent in all lakes but Borden. Because the park is in a transition zone, plant, mammal, and bird species are diverse. A mixed forest of aspen, white spruce, balsam poplar, and jack pine grows on the uplands, whereas black spruce and tamarack grow in lower, wetter

areas. Beavers are common—look for their ponds on the north side of Laurier Lake. Other resident mammals include porcupines, white-tailed deer, coyotes, and, during berry season, black bears. Birds are abundant, especially waterfowl and shorebirds. A 1.5-kilometer (0.9-mile) interpretive trail starts at the day-use area at the northeast corner of Ross Lake. Fishing is best for northern pike, perch, and pickerel.

Within the park are two campgrounds with a total of more than 200 sites. **Ross Lake Campground** has 149 powered sites on six short loops around the south and eastern shore of the lake. Coin-operated showers are located between loops A and B. Whitney Lakes Campground is smaller and has no showers but does have power hookups. A trail along the shore links both campgrounds. Sites are $15–21, and no reservations are taken. Both are open May–mid-October.

Frog Lake

On April 2, 1885, a band of Cree led by Chief Big Bear massacred nine whites in a remote Hudson's Bay Company post on Frog Lake. It was an act of desperation on the part of the Cree. The great buffalo herds had been devastated, and the fur trade was coming to an end. Big Bear had been forced into signing land treaties to prevent his people from starving. Life on reserves didn't suit the nomadic Cree, and they yearned to return to the old ways. Exactly what sparked the massacre remains unknown, but word of confrontations farther east may have encouraged the Cree. Historians believe the natives originally planned to take hostages, but when Tom Quinn, the post's Indian agent, refused native orders, a shooting spree took place.

The site is marked by a small graveyard and a series of interpretive panels outlining the events leading up to the massacre. To get there from Whitney Lakes, continue east on Highway 646 to its junction with Highway 897. Follow Highway 897 north to the small hamlet of Frog Lake. At the Frog Lake General Store, head east for three kilometers (1.9 miles) to a slight rise, then south at the crest.

To Lloydminster

From Frog Lake, get back on Highway 646 and follow it east to Highway 17 at the native community of **Onion Lake.** Highway 17 parallels the border 26 kilometers (16 miles) south to Lloydminster.

NORTHEAST TOWARD COLD LAKE

Highway 28A leaves Ashmont and bisects Upper and Lower Mann Lakes (best fishing is in Upper Mann Lake on the *south* side of the road).

Glendon

Twenty-five kilometers (15.5 miles) farther east is a turnoff to Glendon. This village's claim to fame takes the cake, or actually the pyrogy—it has the **world's largest pyrogy.** This important part of the Ukrainian diet (something like boiled potato- or onion-filled ravioli) can be sampled next to Pyrogy Park (free camping) in the Pyrogy Park Cafe, opposite the Pyrogy Motel (780/635-3002; from $65 s or d) on Pyrogy Drive.

Bonnyville

Originally called St. Louis de Moose Lake, this town of 5,500 is an agriculture center surrounded by many good fishing and swimming lakes, including **Moose Lake,** to the west, and **Muriel Lake,** to the south. The town is situated on the north shore of **Jessie Lake,** where more than 300 species of waterfowl and shorebirds have been recorded. Spring and fall are the best viewing times, although many species are present year-round, nesting in the marshes and aspen parkland surrounding the lake. Numerous viewing platforms, linked by the **Wetlands Nature Trail,** are scattered along Lakeshore Drive and Highway 41.

All of Bonnyville's tourist facilities, including motels, are along the main highway. The **Visitor Information Centre** (Hwy. 28, 780/826-3252, 9 A.M.–8 P.M. Mon.–Fri. and 10 A.M.–6 P.M. Sat.–Sun. in summer) is at the west end of town.

Moose Lake Provincial Park

Moose Lake is a large, shallow body of water west of Bonnyville between Highways 28A and 660. One of Alberta's earliest trading posts was built in 1789 on the shore of Moose Lake by Angus Shaw, of the North West Company. All that remains of the post is a pile of rocks and a depression just west of Moose Lake River (which forms the park's western boundary). In 1870, a smallpox epidemic wiped out the local Cree—they're buried on the west side of Deadman's Point. Access to the lake is possible from many directions, but the 736-hectare (1,820-acre) provincial park is on the lake's north shore. All but Deadman's Point has been affected by fire and is reforested with jack pine and dense forests of aspen and birch. Ground squirrels and coyotes are common, and black bears occasionally wander through. The park's namesake moose, however, are long gone. The lakeshore is a good place to explore, with trails leading either way from the day-use area to good sandy beaches. Another trail leads to the tip of Deadman's Point and to a bog that is home to many species of birds. Fishing in the lake is best for northern pike, perch, and walleye. The small campground has 59 sites on two loops, both of which have access to the beach; unserviced sites $15, powered sites $21. It's open mid-May–mid-September.

COLD LAKE

At the end of Highway 28, a little less than 300 kilometers (186 miles) northeast of Edmonton, is Cold Lake (pop. 12,500). The town is comprised of two very distinct communities. The area you'll want to visit is Cold Lake North, on the south shore of Alberta's seventh-largest lake. This historic town has a large marina and is close to Cold Lake Provincial Park. The town that is still marked on many maps as Medley—now part of Cold Lake South—is, in fact, only the name of the post office at **4 Wing Cold Lake,** Canada's largest air force base. Over 5,000 military personnel and their families live on the base, using an air-weapons range that occupies a large tract of wilderness to the north. The other part of Cold Lake South is a large service and residential area formerly known as Grand Centre. At the town's main intersection is a CF-104 Starfighter donated by the base in recognition of the ties between the communities.

Although the military has been present for over half a century, it is the **Cold Lake Oil Sands** that hold the key to the region's economic future. The heavy oil found north of Cold Lake is similar to that of the Athabasca Oil Sands at Fort McMurray, but the extraction process is different. The oil-rich sands lie in 50-meter-thick (160-foot-thick) underground reservoirs, making surface mining impractical. Instead, steam is pumped into the reservoirs, thinning out the tarlike bitumen, which is then pumped to the surface and piped to Edmonton. This process, known as "steam injection," is still in its developmental stages and is very expensive, but many of the major players in the North American oil market have leases around Cold Lake.

Alberta's Seventh-Largest Lake

Cold Lake is part of what was once a much

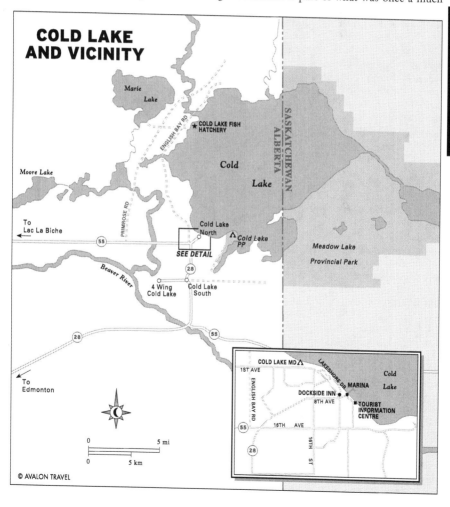

larger lake, a remnant of the last ice age. Today the lake is approximately 22 kilometers (13.6 miles) wide, 27 kilometers (13.6 miles) long, and reaches depths of 100 meters (330 foot). Its surface is frozen for five months of the year and doesn't break up until early May; the tackle shop at the marina has a sheet pinned to the wall showing breakup dates for the last 50 years. Fishing in the lake is best for northern pike, lake trout, and walleye.

Cold Lake North, on the south shore, is the center of most activity on the lake. The 250-berth **marina** (at the end of the main street) provides a home for **Cap'n Ronn Charters** (780/812-8895), which offers varying packages in a modern seven-meter (23-foot) boat. Charters are from $80 per hour for up to four people, but it's least expensive for a full day of guided fishing ($525). The best beaches are on the northwestern shore of the lake at **English Bay. Kinosoo Beach,** along Lakeshore Drive, is also popular.

The **Cold Lake Fish Hatchery** (780/639-4087) is one of five facilities in Alberta where fish hatched at Calgary's Sam Livingston Fish Hatchery are raised to stock lakes throughout the province. It's open for self-guided tours 10 A.M.–3 P.M. daily. To get there, take Highway 55 eight kilometers (five miles) west of Cold Lake, take Primrose Road 15 kilometers (nine miles) north, then head two kilometers (1.2 miles) east.

Cold Lake Provincial Park

This 5,855-hectare (14,470-acre) park is on a low isthmus of land east of town along 16th Avenue. Although the beaches are much nicer on the northwestern shore of the lake, fishing is excellent here, and the park holds many interesting places to explore. A diversity of plant species grows in the park, thanks to its location in a transition zone between boreal forest and aspen parkland. Balsam fir and white spruce dominate the northern end of the peninsula, whereas stands of aspen and birch can be found to the south. The dominant natural feature of the park is **Hall's Lagoon,** on the northwest side of the isthmus. The lagoon is very shallow,

and thick vegetation lines its banks. This is the best place for viewing birdlife, with an observation platform and identification boards set up for bird-watchers. More than 40 species of mammals also inhabit the area, including muskrat, mink, water shrew, and moose. Within the park are many short hiking trails, most radiating from the campground and day-use area. The campground has coin-operated showers, firewood, a beach, summer interpretive programs, and is open May–October; unserviced sites $18, powered sites $24.

Accommodations and Camping

Within walking distance of the marina is the **Dockside Inn** (1002 8th Ave., 780/639-3030 or 877/639-3038; $75 s, $85 d), with tolerable air-conditioned rooms, an Internet kiosk, and a Laundromat. Much nicer is the **Lakeland Inn** (5411 55th St., 708/594-3311 or 877/594-3311; $120 s, $138 d), where each of the 121 rooms has wireless Internet, comfortable beds, and air-conditioning. Dining options include a café, lounge, and restaurant.

Along 1st Avenue, past Kinosoo Beach, is the **Cold Lake MD Campground** (780/639-4121, mid-May–mid-Sept., $22–24), popular with families who stay the summer. Other options for campers are located east at **Cold Lake Provincial Park** (780/639-3341, May–Oct., $18–24) and west along Highway 55, where numerous gravel roads head north to primitive campgrounds (kitchen shelters, firewood, pit toilets); the best of the bunch is at **English Bay,** on the northwest shore of Cold Lake.

Information and Services

Housed in a two-story building on the highway through Cold Lake South is **Cold Lake Information Centre** (780/594-4497 or 800/840-6140, www.coldlake.com, 9 A.M.–9 P.M. Mon.–Fri., 10 A.M.–6 P.M. Sat.–Sun. May–Aug.).

In Cold Lake North, the **post office** is at 913 8th Avenue. The only launderette is at the Husky gas station in Cold Lake South. **Cold Lake Health Centre** (314 25th St., 780/639-3322) is through Cold Lake North to the west.

LAC LA BICHE

The historic town of Lac La Biche (pop. 2,600) is located on the southern flanks of the boreal forest, 225 kilometers (140 miles) northeast of Edmonton. The town itself has little of interest, but nearby you'll find a restored mission, two interesting provincial parks, many excellent fishing lakes, and a gravel road that may or may not get you to Fort McMurray.

The town lies on a divide that separates the Athabasca River System, which drains into the Arctic Ocean, from the Churchill River System, which drains into Hudson Bay. The historic Portage La Biche, across this strip of land, was a vital link in the transcontinental route taken by the early fur traders. Voyageurs would paddle up the Beaver River from the east to Beaver Lake and portage the five kilometers (3.1 miles) to Lac La Biche, from where passage could be made to the rich fur-trapping regions along the Athabasca River. In 1798, David Thompson built Red Deer Lake House for the North West Company at the southeast end of the lake. Soon after, Peter Fidler built Greenwich House nearby for the Hudson's Bay Company. By the early 1820s, this northern route across the continent was virtually abandoned for a shorter route along the North Saskatchewan River via Edmonton House. The mission is the best place to learn about the town's colorful past, but you can also get a taste at lakeside **McArthur Place** (Churchill Dr., 780/623-4323), which is a replica of the Lac La Biche Inn that once stood on the same site. Now functioning primarily as the town office, it also holds an information center, historical displays, and a stuffed cougar. Out front, a paved walking trail leads along the shoreline to a statue of explorer extraordinaire David Thompson.

Lac La Biche Mission

The mission was established beside the Hudson's Bay Company post in 1853 and was moved to its present site, 11 kilometers (6.8 miles) northwest of Lac La Biche, in 1855. It became a base for priests who had missions along the Athabasca, Peace, and Mackenzie Rivers

and was used as a supply depot for voyageurs still using the northern trade route. The parish expanded, adding a sawmill, a gristmill, a printing press, and a boat-building yard. Today, the original buildings still stand, and services take place each Sunday in the church. A free, guided tour takes one hour, or you can wander around the buildings yourself (780/623-3274, 10 A.M.–5 P.M. daily mid-May–early Sept., adult $5, senior $4.25, child $3.50).

Accommodations and Camping

La Biche Inn (101st Ave., 780/623-4427 or 888/884-8886, $65 s, $75 d) has a restaurant and a nightclub where the disc jockey sits in a big rig. The closest campgrounds are east and north of town in the Sir Winston Churchill and Lakeland Provincial Parks. **Fish 'N Friends** (3 km/1.9 miles east and a similar distance south off Hwy. 36, 780/623-9222, www.fish-nfriends.com, mid-May–Oct., $22–25) is a full-service RV park with a large marina, boat rentals, a general store stocked with fishing tackle, and barbecues, perfect for cooking up freshly caught walleye.

VICINITY OF LAC LA BICHE
Sir Winston Churchill Provincial Park

Located on the largest of nine islands in Lac La Biche, this unique 239-hectare (590-acre) park was linked to the mainland in 1968 by a 2.5-kilometer (1.6-mile) causeway. A road around the island leads through a lush, old-growth coniferous forest. The trees on the island are much larger than those found on the mainland as a result of little disturbance from people and no major fires in more than 300 years. As they come to the end of their 65-year life span, the aspen and poplar that dominate younger boreal forests are replaced by balsam fir. Many fir trees are 150 years old and reach a height of 23 meters (74 feet). Along the loop road, short trails lead to sandy beaches (the best are on the northeast side of the island), marshes rich with birdlife, and a bird-viewing platform where a mounted telescope lets you watch white pelicans and double-crested cormorants resting on a gravel bar. A campground (780/623-4144, May–mid-Oct., $23–26) with showers includes a few powered sites on the south side of the island.

Lakeland Provincial Park and Recreation Area

Encompassing 60,000 hectares (148,000 acres) of boreal forest that is mostly in its natural state, this park and adjacent recreation area are a wildlife-watcher's paradise that includes 11 major lakes. Deer, moose, beavers, red foxes, lynx, coyotes, a few wolves and black bears, and more than 200 species of birds can be spotted in the area. A colony of great blue herons, Alberta's largest wading bird, lives at **Pinehurst Lake,** 27 kilometers (17 miles) off Highway 55. Fishing in the lakes is excellent for northern pike and walleye. Those with their own canoes can get out on the water for a real wilderness experience. Several routes access the two areas; head east from Lac La Biche or north from Highway 55.

Fort McMurray and the Remote Northeast

It's a long drive up a one-way highway to reach Fort McMurray, 450 kilometers (280 miles) north of Edmonton, but it's far from a dead-end town. This city is a modern-day boom-town that revolves around the Athabasca Oil Sands, the world's greatest known deposit of oil. The city is awash with money, and workers spending it, but on a larger scale, the financial impact on the province and country is mind-blowing. So if you're not a construction worker or oilman, why should you make the long trek north? Actual "sights" are oil sands related (tours through the mining operations are very popular), but nowhere in the world has so much economic development ever been concentrated in one place, which makes simply being there an interesting study in socioeconomics.

To Fort McMurray

For many years, the only way to get to Fort McMurray was by airplane or the Muskeg Express, a rail service to Edmonton. Today, a paved highway (Highway 63), as good as any in the province, has replaced the rail line. It parallels, but never crosses, the Athabasca River, which cuts deeply into the boreal forest, covering the entire northern half of the province. From the highway's southern terminus (at the junction of Highway 55, between Lac La Biche and Athabasca) to Fort McMurray, only two small communities are found. The first is **Wandering River,** a small lumber and service town with gas, a motel, and a 24-hour restaurant. The Alberta government maintains primitive campgrounds 13, 58, and 76 kilometers (8, 31, and 47 miles) north of Wandering River. Each has a water source, pit toilets, kitchen shelter, and firewood; $11 per night. Along the route are many roadside fens and areas ravished by fire, where the cycle of natural reforestation has begun.

Mariana Lake, a little more than halfway to Fort McMurray, has the same services as Wandering River. Just south of town is **Mariana Lake Recreation Area,** which, although beside the highway, has a good campground; $11 per night.

History

In 1870, Henry Moberly opened a trading post on the Athabasca River and named it after the chief factor of the Hudson's Bay Company, William McMurray. The post quickly gained popularity as a transportation hub and for trading with Cree and Chipewyan natives. The natives first reported oil oozing from the sand here, but it took a long time for anyone to gain commercial success from extracting it. For the first half of the 20th century, the town experienced little growth. But in 1964, the first oil-sands plant was built, and 10 years later a second company began operation. Today the city has an air of permanence about it. As new

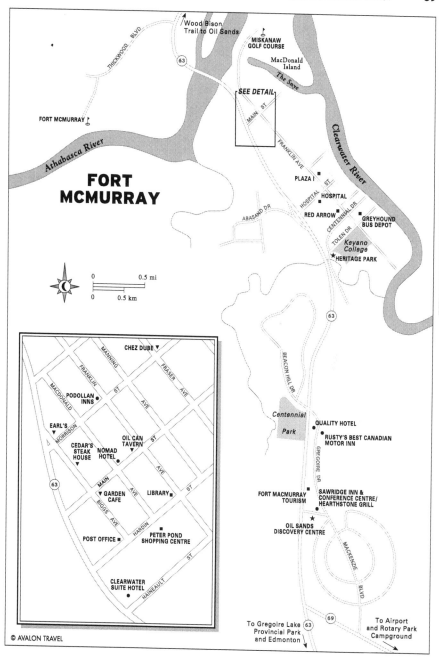

FORT MCMURRAY

Wood Bison Trail to Oil Sands

THICKWOOD BLVD

63

MISKANAW GOLF COURSE

MacDonald Island

The Snye

SEE DETAIL

MAIN ST

FRANKLIN AVE

Clearwater River

FORT MCMURRAY

Athabasca River

PLAZA I ST

HOSPITAL DR   HOSPITAL

ABASAND DR   RED ARROW   CENTENNIAL DR   GREYHOUND BUS DEPOT

TOLEN DR

Keyano College

HERITAGE PARK

63

BEACON HILL DR

Centennial Park

QUALITY HOTEL

RUSTY'S BEST CANADIAN MOTOR INN

GREGOIRE DR

FORT MACMURRAY TOURISM   SAWRIDGE INN & CONFERENCE CENTRE/ HEARTHSTONE GRILL

OIL SANDS DISCOVERY CENTRE

MACKENZIE BLVD

0   0.5 mi
0   0.5 km

63   69

To Gregoire Lake 63 Provincial Park and Edmonton   To Airport and Rotary Park Campground

Detail

CHEZ DUBE

MANNING ST

FRASER AVE

FRANKLIN ST

MACDONALD

PODOLLAN INNS

EARL'S

MORRISON

CEDAR'S STEAK HOUSE

OIL CAN TAVERN

NOMAD HOTEL

ST

AVE

AVE

ST

63

MAIN AVE

GARDEN CAFE

LIBRARY

BIGGS AVE

HARDIN

PETER POND SHOPPING CENTRE

POST OFFICE

ST

CLEARWATER SUITE HOTEL   HAINEAULT

© AVALON TRAVEL

subdivisions are carved into the boreal forest, suburbs of respectable three-bedroom homes have sprung up, and downtown looks similar to hundreds of midsize cities across Canada. The city is now part of the Region of Wood Buffalo, North America's largest municipality, at 67,104 square kilometers (25,900 square miles).

ATHABASCA OIL SANDS

Only 800 billion barrels of conventional crude oil are known to remain on this entire planet, but the Athabasca Oil Sands, north of Fort McMurray, hold twice that amount in a single reserve. The accepted estimate is that only 315 billion barrels (more than is present in all of Saudi Arabia) of the total field are recoverable using the technology of today. Still, that's a lot of oil, and the math is easy—it will take 100 years to extract just 20 percent of the recoverable oil. Within 500 years, someone will probably have figured out a way to get at the other 80 percent of the deposit. The oil is not conventional oil but a heavy oil, commonly called bitumen, that must be processed to produce a lighter, more useful oil. Of the many crucial differences between conventional oil reserves and the heavy, tarlike oil sands of Fort McMurray, none is more important than the associated costs. Operating costs for extracting and processing the oil sands' bitumen currently run at $12 per barrel, compared to Middle East crude, which can be pumped out of the ground for just $1 a barrel. Benefits include no exploration costs for oil sands and that the processing plants are connected to the insatiable U.S. market by pipelines. Still, with improvements in technology, world supplies of conventional crude slowly being depleted, and oil estimated to be selling for US$100 a barrel in the not too distant future, the oil sands of Fort McMurray are the focus of big oil companies with *big* money—some $100 billion worth of planned development is under way to complement existing infrastructure.

The Players

Massive mining operations punctuate the remote boreal forest north and east of Fort McMurray. **Suncor** began production in 1967 after taking over the company that had initiated mining in the area three years earlier. The Suncor operation became the world's first commercially successful oil-sands plant. It has been expanding its operation, having merged with Petro-Canada in 2009 to create Canada's second-largest company. Suncor pumps around 230,000 barrels of oil per day and has 15 million barrels still to extract. Established in 1978, **Syncrude,** the world's largest producer of synthetic crude oil, is also expanding its Fort McMurray operations. The company has spent $12 billion in the first decade of the 21st century to increase production to 350,000 barrels per day, increasing to 200 million barrels per year by 2015. In the lead up to pumping its first oil in 2002, Shell Canada's **Albian Sands** site was the world's largest construction project, employing up to 15,000 workers on-site at any one time. **Canadian Natural Resources** is one of many companies starting from scratch in the oil sands. Their Horizon site, slated to be pumping 230,000 barrels of oil per day by 2012, is costing $30 billion, making it the most ambitious construction project ever undertaken anywhere in the world by a private company.

All told, around $50 billion have been spent on oil-sands development since the mid-1990s, with the major players in the industry having collaborated on a development proposal that guarantees a combined regional investment of a further $70 billion over the next 15 years. The current total production rate of 1.3 million barrels a day is expected to increase to three million barrels by 2020.

The Process

As the name implies, the deposits are of highly compacted sand containing heavy oil or bitumen. The sands are mined in two different ways—deposits close to the surface are strip-mined, while the oil deeper down is extracted in situ (using steam injection). In the case of surface deposits, the size of the machinery used to scrape off the surface layer of muskeg and excavate the oil sands below it is mind-boggling. Syncrude's walking draglines are the largest pieces of land-bound machinery in the world. Each moves slowly, dropping buckets as large as a two-car garage into the ground and dragging them back on a boom the length of a football field. The process continues around the clock, with a constant stream of 170-ton heavy haulers taking the overburden to reclamation sites and the oil sands to conveyor belts bound for the processing plants.

Extracting oil sands that lie deep below the earth's surface is very costly. A simplified explanation of the process is that the fields are tapped by parallel wells. Steam is injected in one, loosening then liquefying and separating the oil from the sand. A second lower well extracts the resulting oil. Around 80 percent of known deposits will require this type of extraction technique.

Once on the surface, it must be chemically altered to produce a lighter, more useful oil. This process—in stark contrast to other operations where the oil is simply brought to the surface and shipped or piped around the world—requires an enormous amount of machinery and labor. Hot water and steam are used to separate the sand from the bitumen, which is then diluted with naphtha to make it flow more easily. The bitumen is heated to 500°C (930°F), producing vapors that, when cooled, condense at three levels. The sulfur and the gases produced during the process are all drawn off and put to use, but the liquid products are the most precious. By blending them and increasing the hydrogen content of the mix to make it "lighter," a high-quality synthetic crude oil is produced. This oil is piped to Edmonton and distributed around North America for use in vehicles, airplanes, and derivative products such as plastics.

The People

In 1974, the population of Fort McMurray was just 1,500. Today it stands at 75,000, having been rising by almost 10 percent annually for the last decade. While the current permanent population is quoted at 75,000, this doesn't take into account the tens of thousands of temporary contract workers living in modular camps up at the actual oil sands. Factor these folks in, and you have Alberta's third-largest city.

Workers are attracted to Fort McMurray for one reason: money. Local dishwashers make $50,000 a year, entry-level workers at the mines make over six figures, and the exotic dancers in town make the workers happy. With the super-high wages paid in the oil fields, downtown businesses are chronically understaffed, so much so that many offer retention awards or provide hiring bonuses to employees who find new workers. Up in the oil fields themselves, companies like Canadian Natural Resources have found it easiest to fly its construction workers into a private airstrip by charter plane from Edmonton. The province of Newfoundland and Labrador is a big supplier of labor, so much so that there are direct flights from Fort McMurray to St. John's, as well as a "Newfie" music hour on the local radio station and even the only Mary Brown's (a fast-food chain) outside of that eastern province.

The downside to high wages is a high cost of living. Incredibly, Fort McMurray currently has the hottest market in Canada, with trailers selling from $300,000 and single-family homes averaging $500,000. The rental vacancy rate is generally quoted at zero percent, and if something does come up, you can expect to pay around $1,800 per month for a one-bedroom apartment.

SIGHTS
Oil Sands Discovery Centre

For an insight into the history, geology, and technology of the Athabasca Oil Sands mining process, head to this large interpretive center (515 Mackenzie Blvd., 780/743-7167, 9 A.M.–5 P.M. daily mid-May–Aug., 10 A.M.–4 P.M. Tues.–Sun. the rest of the year, adult $6, senior $5, child $4). Start your visit by watching *Quest for Energy,* a multimedia, big-screen presentation about the industry that has grown around the resource. The center

NORTHERN ALBERTA

houses an interesting collection of machinery and has interactive displays, hands-on exhibits, and interpretive presentations. Outside is the Industrial Equipment Garden, where an older-style bucket-wheel excavator and other machinery are displayed. To move the excavator to this site, it had to be disassembled, with some sections requiring a 144-wheel, 45-meter-long (150-foot-long) trailer for the 45-kilometer (28-mile) trip from the mine.

◖ Syncrude and Suncor Plant Tours

Touring the oil-sands plants is the best way to experience the operation firsthand. The scope of the developments is overwhelming, while the size of the machinery is almost inconceivable. Two companies—Syncrude and Suncor—are involved in tour programs offered through **Fort McMurray Tourism** (780/791-4336 or 800/565-3947, www.fortmcmurraytourism. com). Tours of the Syncrude site depart at 9 A.M. every Saturday in June, Wednesday–Saturday July–August, and Friday–Saturday in

September. The Suncor tour departs at 1 P.M. Sunday–Monday in June, Sunday–Tuesday July–August. Regardless of which tour you choose, the itinerary is similar. Departing from the Oil Sands Discovery Centre, the tours involve a bus ride north with stops at Wood Bison Trail Gateway and the Giants of Mining display, and then a tour of either the Syncrude or Suncor sites, with time set aside to get out of the bus at a lookout point. The round-trip takes around four hours. Tour cost is adult $35, senior and youth $30, which includes entry to the Discovery Centre and to Heritage Park, a historic village. Children under 12 are not permitted, and a security check is made before departure (have a photo ID ready). To join a tour, you *must* make advance reservations. (The tourism office has put together some accommodation/tour packages that are an excellent deal—around $180 per person for two nights' accommodation and a tour.)

Wood Bison Trail

Driving north from the city on Highway 63

oil-sands plant tour, Fort McMurray

© ANDREW HEMPSTEAD

gives you a chance to view the mining operations (albeit at a distance), plus make a few interesting stops. Up to 40,000 vehicles a day traverse this route, including 400 buses filled with workers, so be prepared for a lot of traffic.

Make your first stop 27 kilometers (17 miles) north of Fort McMurray at the **Wood Bison Trail Gateway,** where there is an impressive wood bison sculpture made from oil sands. Also on display is a 100-million-year-old cypress tree found fossilized in the oil sands. This pullout is also the starting point for the **Matcheetawin Discovery Trails,** two interpretive loops over a reclaimed mine now covered in a mixed forest of aspen and spruce. The longer of the two passes a lookout over the Syncrude development. Continuing north three kilometers (1.9 miles), you'll find a turn to the left that climbs to a viewpoint over a herd of 300 bison. The road then parallels a reclamation pond to the **Giants of Mining** exhibit, comprising some of the original machinery used in oil-sands development. This is the beginning of the Syncrude spread, and as the road loops around the pond, you begin to get a feel for the scope of the operation. Around 55 kilometers (34 miles) from Fort McMurray, the road forks. To the left is Fort McKay, and to the right Highway 63 crosses the Athabasca River and continues 10 kilometers (6.2 miles) to a dock. Here, supplies such as petroleum and building materials are loaded onto barges and transported downstream (north) to remote communities such as Fort Chipewyan.

This is the end of the summer road. Between December and March, a winter road is built over the frozen muskeg and river 225 kilometers (140 miles) to Fort Chipewyan and up the Slave River to Fort Smith in the Northwest Territories.

Heritage Park
A two-hectare (five-acre) village, Heritage Park (1 Tolen Dr., 780/791-7575, 9 A.M.–5 P.M. Mon.–Sat., 9:30 A.M.–5 P.M. Sun. mid-June–Aug., adult $8, senior and child $5) is made up of historic buildings linked by a boardwalk and houses artifacts that reflect the importance of fishing, trapping, and transportation to the city. Other displays include boats used on the river, a Northern Alberta Railway passenger car, and an early log mission, while another tells the story of local bush pilots.

Gregoire Lake Provincial Park
Southeast of the city 29 kilometers (18 miles) is Gregoire Lake, the only accessible lake in the Fort McMurray area. The 690-hectare (1,700-acre) park on the lake's west shore is a typical boreal forest of mixed woods and black-spruce bogs. Many species of waterfowl nest on the lake, and mammals such as moose and black bears are relatively common. Some short hiking trails wind through the park, and canoes are rented in the day-use area, which also has a sandy beach and playground.

RECREATION
Golf
Miskanaw Golf Course (north of downtown on MacDonald Island, 780/791-0070, $62) is a challenging 6,650-yard layout with plenty of hazards. More challenging is **Fort McMurray Golf Club** (off Thickwood Blvd., 780/743-5577, $75) with narrow tree-lined fairways.

Swimming and Fitness Centers
The **MacDonald Island Recreation Complex** (McDonald Island, 780/791-0070, 8 A.M.–11 P.M. daily) has a modern exercise room, tennis courts, squash courts, and a swimming pool.

ENTERTAINMENT
The Arts
It's possible to find some big-city culture if you search it out. **Keyano College** (8115 Franklin Ave., 780/791-4990, www.keyano.ca) is a major learning center, with courses as diverse as heavy-machinery operations and holistic healing. **Keyano Theatre** puts on a season of live performances September–May at the college, while a small art gallery (780/791-8979,

NORTHERN ALBERTA

© ANDREW HEMPSTEAD

Keyano College

noon–2 P.M. Mon.–Fri., 1–4 P.M. Sat. Sept.–May) opens during the school year.

Nightlife

As you'd expect, Fort McMurray has dozens of wild, noisy bars filled with workers who have more money than they know what to do with. Downtown, the **Oil Can Tavern,** in the Oil Sands Hotel (10007 Franklin Ave., 780/743-2211), is legendary as a hard-drinking pub with weekend country or rock-and-roll bands. Also in this hotel are a regular nightclub and a strip joint. A more subdued option would be to relax with a quiet drink on the leather sofas of the **Pillar Pub** at Podollan Inns (10131 Franklin Ave., 780/790-2000). South of downtown, the **Sawridge Inn and Conference Centre** (530 Mackenzie Blvd., 780/791-7900) has a pleasant lounge overlooking an indoor pool, or stop by the **Lions Den Pub** at the Quality Hotel (424 Gregoire Dr., 780/791-7200) to shoot some pool.

ACCOMMODATIONS AND CAMPING

High demand dictates there are no bargains in Fort McMurray, and in fact just getting a room

can be difficult. Therefore, if you're planning to stay indoors, it's imperative you book your Fort McMurray accommodations as far in advance as possible. Check with Fort McMurray Tourism (780/791-4336 or 800/565-3947, www.fortmcmurraytourism.com) for accommodation/tour package deals.

$100-150

Rusty's Best Canadian Motor Inn (385 Gregoire Dr., 780/791-4646, www.bestcdn. com, $94 s, $104 d) is one of a bunch of properties four kilometers (2.5 miles) south of downtown near the visitors center. All rooms have a fridge and some have kitchens, or dine in the hotel restaurant or lounge.

Across the road from Rusty's is the **Quality Hotel** (424 Gregoire Dr., 780/791-7200 or 800/582-3273). You'll do no better for value than the midsized Standard rooms ($149 s or d), or splurge on a Superior room ($219 s or d) that really is superior. On the bottom floor is a restaurant, lounge, and indoor swimming pool.

$150-200

An excellent alternative to the hotel options is

Chez Dube (10102 Fraser Ave., 780/790-2367 or 800/565-0757, www.chezdube.com, $175 s, $190 d), a turreted 14-room bed-and-breakfast surrounded by a well-tended garden that includes colorful flowerpots hanging from the veranda. The rooms each have a pastel color scheme, comfortable beds, en suite bathroom, Wi-Fi, and television. Rates include a full breakfast and use of a games room. It backs onto the riverfront park and is only a few blocks from the main street.

Over $200
Fort McMurray's largest accommodation, with 190 rooms, is the **Sawridge Inn and Conference Centre** (530 Mackenzie Blvd., 780/791-7900 or 800/661-6567, www.sawridge.com, $219–249 s or d). Rooms have all the standard amenities business travelers demand, including wireless Internet, while the city's best breakfast is served each morning in the downstairs restaurant. A lounge is spread around an indoor pool complex.

Downtown, the seven-story **Nomad Hotel & Suites** (10006 MacDonald Ave., 780/791-4770 or 866/650-3678, www.nomadfortmcmurray.com, $219–249 s or d) was last revamped in 2000 (a long time ago for a place whose main customers are construction workers) but remains reasonably well kept. It also has underground parking, an airport shuttle, a café, a reliable Keg Steakhouse restaurant, and a lively bar.

Podollan Inns (10131 Franklin Ave., 780/790-2000 or 888/448-2080, www.podollan.com, $239–319 s or d) is one of the newer downtown hotels. Extra-large guest rooms come with modern conveniences such as cardlock entry and wireless Internet, while downstairs is one of the city's quieter lounges, a restaurant, and heated underground parking.

Even newer (2005) is **Clearwater Suite Hotel** (4 Haineault St., 780/799-7676 or 877/799-7676, www.clearwaterfortmcmurray.com, $259–299 s or d), which is aimed at long-term stays but is the nicest choice right downtown. Guest rooms are modern and come with 32-inch TVs, free Internet access, a

washer/dryer combo, a kitchen, and free light breakfast. It's well worth the few extra dollars for a King Suite.

Campgrounds
Rotary Park Campground (Hwy. 69, 780/790-1581, $20) offers showers, cooking facilities, and powered sites and is open year-round. The park is signposted but easy to miss; turn east along Highway 69 and look for the entrance to the left.

Farther from town is the forested campground at **Gregoire Lake Provincial Park** (19 km/12 miles south on Hwy. 63, then 10 km/6.2 miles east on Hwy. 881, 780/334-2111, unserviced sites $20, powered sites $24), which has 140 fairly private sites, 60 with power hookups. Facilities include showers, firewood, and watercraft rentals.

FOOD
Even though wages in Fort McMurray are twice the national average, it doesn't mean the locals have fancy tastes. In fact, the city lacks any really good restaurants at all, with all the business going to fast-food restaurants and family-oriented chains. Also, local eateries find it very hard to find staff, which translates to service that is often adequate at best. It also means shortened hours simply because there is no one to work.

For breakfast, it's hard to pass up recommending the **Hearthstone Grill** (Sawridge Inn and Conference Centre, 530 Mackenzie Blvd., 780/791-7900, from 6:30 A.M. daily), which has a surprisingly good buffet at an even better price—just $12, including coffee. Adding to the appeal is an open dining space that is stylish and welcoming. Lunch is also served buffet-style, while dinner mains start at $17.50.

The **Keg Steakhouse** (Nomad Hotel, 10006 MacDonald Ave., 780/791-4770, 11 A.M.–midnight Mon.–Sat., 4–11 P.M. Sun.) is part of a Canadian chain renowned for fine cuts of Alberta beef served up in a stylish family-restaurant atmosphere. You can't go wrong by ordering the prime rib with horseradish sauce, boiled vegetables, and a roast potato ($18–25), or go creative and try the teriyaki sirloin ($28). **Earl's** (9802 Morrison St., 780/791-3275, lunch and dinner daily) has a similar smart atmosphere and wide-ranging menu. A few pastas are under $17, and steak ranges $20–28.

Cedar's Steakhouse (10020 Biggs Ave., 780/743-1717, from 4 P.M. daily) is a dimly lit room attached to a bar. Locals may tell you this is where they go for a splurge, but in reality the food is no better than at the upscale chains like Earl's and the Keg. Expect to pay around $25 for a T-bone with salad and potato.

INFORMATION AND SERVICES

Fort McMurray Tourism (780/791-4336 or 800/565-3947, www.fortmcmurraytourism. com) does an excellent job of promoting the city to the world. They operate an information center south of downtown (8 A.M.–5 P.M. Mon.–Fri. and 9 A.M.–5 P.M. Sat.–Sun. June–Aug., 8:30 A.M.–4:30 P.M. Mon.–Fri. Sept.–May), just north of the Oil Sands Discovery Centre. In addition to having a wealth of information on the city, the organization represents many northern fly-in fishing lodges and offers overnight accommodation packages.

The **post office** is at 9521 Franklin Avenue. **Fort Laundromat** (Plaza I on Franklin Ave.) is open 9 A.M.–9 P.M. daily. **Fort McMurray Public Library** is housed in a large rust-colored building (9907 Franklin Ave., 780/743-7800, 5–9 P.M. Mon., 10 A.M.–5 P.M. Tues.–Wed., 1–9 P.M. Thurs., 10 A.M.–5 P.M. Fri.–Sat., 1–5 P.M. Sun.). It has free Internet access, or pay a few bucks an hour at **Frogz** (8706 Franklin Ave., 780/743-3839, 3–10 P.M. Tues.–Sun.).

For emergencies, contact **Fort McMurray Regional Hospital** (7 Hospital St., 780/791-6161) or the **RCMP** (780/799-8888).

GETTING THERE AND AROUND

Getting There

It's a long 450-kilometer (280-mile) drive up to Fort McMurray on a highway that is regarded

Fort McMurray Public Library

© ANDREW HEMPSTEAD

as one of the most dangerous in the province (mostly due to the high volume of traffic), so many people prefer to fly. The **airport** is nine kilometers (5.6 miles) south, then six kilometers (3.7 miles) east of downtown. **Air Canada** (888/247-2262, www.aircanada.com), **WestJet** (800/538-5696, www.westjet.com), and **Air Mikisew** (780/743-8218 or 888/268-7112, www.airmikisew.com) fly daily between Edmonton and Fort McMurray, with Air Mikisew departing from the centrally located Edmonton City Centre Airport. Once at the airport, you'll find hotel phones, rental cars (make sure you have a reservation), and a line of cabs charging $35 to get downtown.

Greyhound (8220 Manning Ave., 780/791-3664, www.greyhound.ca) has service three times daily to Edmonton. **Red Arrow** (8217 Franklin Ave., 800/232-1958, www.redarrow.ca) offers a more luxurious service than Greyhound, with fewer stops, more legroom, and free coffee and snacks. Either way, it's a five-hour trip to Edmonton.

Getting Around

Wood Buffalo Transit (780/743-4157) is a

local bus service to outlying suburbs and the Oil Sands Discovery Centre. Buses run seven days a week, and travel costs $1.75 per sector; seniors ride free. From downtown, a cab costs $15 to the Oil Sands Discovery Centre and $35 to the airport. Taxi companies include **Access Taxi** (780/799-3333), **Sun Taxi** (780/743-5050), and **United Class Cabs** (780/743-1234). The following car rentals are available in town, and all have airport counters: **Avis** (780/743-4773), **Budget** (780/743-8215), **Hertz** (780/743-4047), and **National** (780/743-6393).

FORT CHIPEWYAN

When the North West Company established a post on the west shore of Lake Athabasca in 1788, what is now Alberta was a wild land with no white settlers. Today, Fort Chipewyan (pop. 1,200), on the site of the original trading post (225 km/140 miles north of Fort McMurray), holds the title of Alberta's most remote community. In summer, the only access is by river

ANDREW HEMPSTEAD

Established in 1874, St. Paul's Anglican Church in Fort Chipewyan is the oldest church in Alberta.

or air. After the winter freeze settles in, a winter road connects the community to the outside world. For fur traders, Fort Chip, as it's best known, was the ideal location for a post. The confluence of the Athabasca and Peace Rivers was nearby, and to the north were the Slave and Mackenzie Rivers. It became a way station for some of Canada's great explorers—Alexander Mackenzie, David Thompson, Simon Fraser, and Sir John Franklin—who rested and replenished supplies at the post.

Sights and Recreation

Set on a south-facing slope overlooking the lake, the town itself is worth a half-day exploration, but most visitors use it as a base for trips into nearby Wood Buffalo National Park and fishing on the lake and nearby rivers. At the east side of town is the **Bicentennial Museum** (Mackenzie Ave., 780/697-3844, 1–5 P.M. Sat.–Sun. year-round, ask at your accommodation for weekday hours, donation), modeled on the original fur-trading post. It is a surprisingly interesting little museum, with highlights including a replica of the original fort, a winter coat made from buffalo hide, old outboard boat motors, handmade moccasins, as well as oddities such as the shell of a Pacific turtle that somehow made its way into Lake Athabasca. You can also purchase handicrafts by local artists. From the back of the museum, a walking trail with interpretive panels leads along the lakefront to a small docking area. Along the way is the 1874 **St. Paul's Anglican Church,** the oldest church in Alberta. The imposing buildings across the bay to the west are part of a Roman Catholic mission.

Athabasca Delta Interpretive Tours (780/697-3521) operates a lodge on Jackfish Lake that is reached by a short boat ride from Fort Chip. The emphasis is on the traditional lifestyle of the local Dene people; activities include wilderness trips, fishing, wildlife viewing, and native cooking. Rates are around $250 per day.

Accommodations and Food

At the time of publication, the future of **Fort**

Chipewyan Lodge (780/697-3679 or 888/686-6333, www.fortchipewyanlodge.com; $150 s or d) was unknown, but it's worth checking out in the future. The 10 basic but comfortable rooms have bathrooms and TV, but don't take full advantage of the setting. The lodge also has a restaurant with great views and a wraparound deck, and an upstairs lounge that is mostly the domain of locals. It takes around 10 minutes to walk downtown from the lodge.

The only other option is **Wah Pun Bed & Breakfast** (780/697-3030, wahpun@telus-planet.net, $105 s, $125 d), a modern log home to the west of town. Owned by former chief Archie Waquan and his wife, Dawn, it's a good place to learn more about local issues. Guest rooms have private bathrooms and phones, while communal areas include a lounge with a pool table and fireplace.

Fort Chipewyan Lodge has a restaurant (8 A.M.–6 P.M. daily, later in summer) with fantastic views over the lake. Unfortunately, the food doesn't live up to the setting—choose from dishes such as pork chops and roast potato ($14) or steak and fries ($18). Downtown across from the municipal office, **Northern Nugget** (780/697-3777, 10 A.M.–7 P.M. daily) doesn't have a sign out front, but inside you'll find a few tables and dishes such as a roast beef sandwich ($10).

Getting There and Around

Operated by the local Cree nation, **Air Mikisew** (780/743-8218 or 888/268-7112, www.airmikisew.com) links Edmonton, Fort McMurray, and Fort Chipewyan with multiple daily scheduled flights. The fare is roughly $200 per sector, inclusive of taxes. Views of the oil sands on these flights are fantastic and will give you an idea of their scope.

Once at the airport, there are usually cabs waiting, including **Tuccaro's Taxi** (780/697-3400), which charges $10 to get into town.

Between mid-December and mid-March, a winter road constructed from Fort McMurray to Fort Smith passes through Fort Chip and is passable by two-wheel-drive vehicles; call 780/697-3778 for road conditions.

◖ WOOD BUFFALO NATIONAL PARK

In the far northeast corner of Alberta is Wood Buffalo National Park, the second-largest national park in the world (the largest is in Greenland). It is accessible by road only through the Northwest Territories or by charter from Fort McMurray. Throughout this 45,000-square-kilometer (17,400-square-mile) chunk of boreal forest, boreal plains, shallow lakes, and bogs flow two major rivers—the Peace and Athabasca. These drain into **Lake Claire,** forming one of the world's largest freshwater deltas. The Peace-Athabasca Delta is a mass of confusing channels, shallow lakes, and sedge meadows, surrounded by a wetland that is a prime wintering range for bison, rich in waterfowl, and home to beavers, muskrats, moose,

WHOOPING CRANES

Through a successful captive-breeding program, the whooping crane, *Grus americana*, has become a symbol of human efforts to protect endangered species in North America. Whoopers, as they are commonly called, have never been prolific. They stand 1.3 meters (four feet), have a wingspan of 2.4 meters (eight feet), and are pure white with long black legs. (They are often confused with the slightly smaller, reddish-brown-colored sandhill crane, which is common in the park.) Their naturally low reproduction rate coupled with severe degradation of their habitat caused their numbers to dip as low as 21 — a single flock that nested in Wood Buffalo National Park — in 1954. Today, the population of the highly publicized and heavily studied flock has increased to more than 200, more than half the number that remain worldwide (most of those remaining are in captivity). The birds nest in a remote area of marshes and bogs in the northern reaches of Wood Buffalo far from human contact, migrating south to the Texas coast each fall.

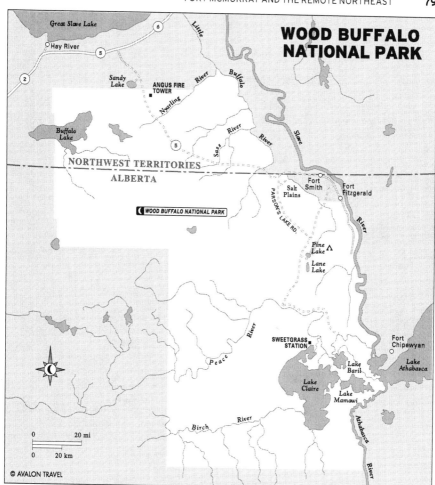

WOOD BUFFALO NATIONAL PARK

© AVALON TRAVEL

lynx, wolves, and black bears. From the delta, the Slave River, which forms the park's eastern boundary, flows north into Great Slave Lake.

Probably best known for being the last natural nesting habitat of the rare whooping crane, the park is also home to the world's largest free-roaming herd of bison. It has extensive salt plains and North America's finest example of gypsum karst topography—a phenomenon created by underground water activity. For all of these reasons, and as an intact example of the boreal forest that once circled the entire Northern Hemisphere, the park was declared a UNESCO World Heritage Site in December 1983.

Sights

The expansive **Salt Plains** in the northeast of the park are one of Wood Buffalo's dominant natural features. Underground water flows through deposits of salt left behind by an ancient saltwater ocean, emerging in the form of salt springs. Large white mounds form at their source, and where the water has evaporated the ground is covered in a fine layer of salt. The best place to view this phenomenon is from the **Salt Plains Overlook,** 35 kilometers (22 miles) west of Fort Smith, then 11 kilometers (6.8 miles) south on Parson's Lake Road. The panoramic view of the plains is spectacular from this spot, but it's worth taking the one-kilometer (0.6-mile) trail to the bottom of the hill.

In the same vicinity, a bedrock of **gypsum karst** underlies much of the park. Gypsum is a soft, white rock that slowly dissolves in water. Underground water here has created large cavities beneath this fragile mantle. This type of terrain is known as karst, and this area is the best example of karst terrain in North America. As the bedrock continues to dissolve, the underground caves enlarge, eventually collapsing under their own weight, forming large depressions known as **sinkholes.** The thousands of sinkholes here vary in size from three meters (10 feet) to 100 meters (330 feet) across. The most accessible large sinkhole is behind the Angus Fire Tower, 150 kilometers (93 miles) west of Fort Smith.

The **Peace-Athabasca Delta** is in a remote part of this remote park and is rarely visited. Getting to the delta requires some planning because no roads access the area. The most popular visitor destination on the delta is **Sweetgrass Station,** located 12 kilometers (7.5 miles) south of the Peace River. The site is on the edge of a vast meadow that extends around the north and west shores of Lake Claire, providing a summer range for most of the park's bison. A cabin with bunks and a woodstove is available for visitors to the area at no charge, although reservations at the park information center are required. The cabin is an excellent base for exploring the meadows around Lake Claire and viewing the abundant wildlife. From Fort Smith, **Northwestern Air** (867/872-2216, www.nwal.ca) charges $480 each way to fly two people and their gear to Sweetgrass Station.

Practicalities

The **Fort Chipewyan Visitor Reception Centre** (126 McDougal Rd., Fort Smith, 867/872-7900, 9 A.M.–5 P.M. Mon.–Fri., plus 1–5 P.M. weekends in summer) offers trail information, a short slide show, and an exhibit room. Another park office (780/697-3662, 8:30 A.M.–5 P.M. Mon.–Fri.) is in Fort Chipewyan. It has an interesting exhibit on the Peace River.

Within the park itself, the only developed facilities are at **Pine Lake,** 60 kilometers (37 miles) south of Fort Smith. The lake has a campground ($14 per night) with pit toilets, covered kitchen shelters, and firewood ($7). On a spit of land jutting into the lake beyond the campground is a picnic area with bugproof shelters. The park staff presents a summer interpretive program at various locations; check the schedule at the park information center or on the campground notice board.

North-Central Alberta

The area immediately north of Edmonton is a varied region that extends north out of the provincial capital's suburbs through rich agricultural land and into the wilderness of the boreal forest. The **Athabasca River** flows southwest to northeast through the region. It is linked to Edmonton by Highway 2, which follows the historic Athabasca Landing Trail—a supply route used by early explorers and traders for travel between the North Saskatchewan and Athabasca River Systems. From Athabasca, Highway 2 heads northwest to the city of Slave Lake, on the southeast shore of Lesser Slave Lake. From there, it continues along the lake's southern shore to High Prairie and into the Peace River Valley. Other major roads in the region include Highway 18, which runs east–west through the southern portion of the region and through the farming and oil towns of Westlock and Barrhead; Highway 33,

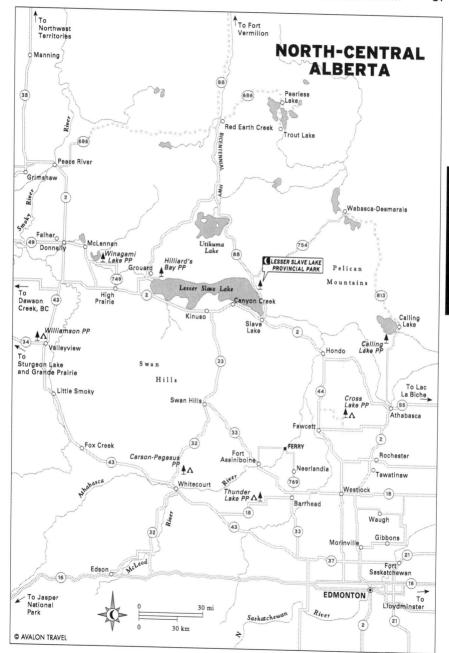

NORTH-CENTRAL ALBERTA

which climbs into the Swan Hills, home to a subspecies of the now-extinct plains grizzly bear; and Highway 43, the main thoroughfare northwest from Edmonton to Grande Prairie. Adventurous souls driving to the Northwest Territories will want to travel the Bicentennial Highway (Highway 88) at least one-way. This gravel road opens up a remote part of the province that is otherwise accessible only by floatplane.

EDMONTON TO ATHABASCA

From downtown Edmonton, Highway 2 (called the St. Albert Trail in the vicinity of Edmonton) heads north into a once-forested land that is now heavily developed as farm and ranch country. The first town north of the city limits is **Morinville,** a farming community founded by French and German settlers more than 100 years ago. **St. Jean Baptiste Church,** built by the town's founders, is an imposing structure that has been declared a Provincial Historic Site.

Athabasca Landing Trail

The Athabasca Landing Trail was a historic trade route plied first by indigenous people and later used by the Hudson's Bay Company to carry goods between Fort Saskatchewan and Athabasca. Bits and pieces of the original trail can still be seen today, interspersed among the small towns and hamlets east of Highway 2.

At one time, the trail passed through **Gibbons,** a small town of 2,800 on the banks of the Sturgeon River. Sites of interest here include **Gibbons Anglican Church,** whose unique interior is shaped like a ship (you can wander through the church anytime), and **Gibbons Museum** (4709 48th Ave., 780/923-2140, 10 A.M.–6 P.M. Wed.–Sun. June–Aug., donation), which features a two-story 1010 log house, a red barn, and an old fire hall. Four kilometers (2.5 miles) north of Gibbons is one of northern Alberta's finest courses, **Goose Hummock Golf Resort** (780/921-2444, $57), a tight layout that is dominated by water hazards that come into play on all but three holes.

Old St. Mary's Ukrainian Catholic Church is 1.5 kilometers (0.9 mile) west of the hamlet of **Waugh.** It was the first church of its denomination to be built north of Edmonton and is adjacent to the original trail. The trail disappears north of Highway 18, but historic markers and buildings are accessible by following gravel roads east through **Tawatinaw** and **Rochester** (look for historic markers and log buildings on the roadside approaching the crest of the first ridge east of these towns).

ATHABASCA AND VICINITY

On the banks of the Athabasca River, 147 kilometers (91 miles) north of Edmonton, this town of 2,500 was probably the most famous of the many communities that formed vital links to the north. Athabasca ("Where There are Reeds," in the language of the Cree) is on a gently sloping hill on the river's south bank, with the steep-sided Muskeg Creek Valley on one side and the Tawatinaw River on the other. Many historic buildings still stand in town, and the surrounding area is pristine wilderness, excellent for fishing, boating, and camping.

History

Athabasca Landing was founded by the Hudson's Bay Company in 1874 on the southernmost bend of the Athabasca River. Goods from the east were shipped to Fort Saskatchewan and transported north along the Athabasca Landing Trail, from where they were distributed throughout northern Canada. A thriving boat-building business began at the landing. Once the paddle wheelers and scows reached their destination along the river system, many were broken up and used for housing; others were loaded with furs for the return journey. Passengers who boarded the paddle wheelers from the landing were from all walks of life—traders, trappers, land speculators, settlers, North West Mounted Police (NWMP), geologists, missionaries, and anyone looking for a new life and adventure in Canada's great northern wilderness. Robert Service, the renowned poet, lived at Athabasca Landing for a time; much of his early work was about trappers and the people of the Athabasca River.

Sights

Although the Hudson's Bay Company buildings have long since disappeared, many later buildings from the days of the paddle wheelers remain. Beside the riverfront information center is an old wooden scow used by early river travelers. Farther along is a railway station, circa 1912, while behind this building is a 1915 steam engine. Up the hill on 48th Street is an old brick schoolhouse, built in 1913. Next door is the library (4716 48th St., 780/675-2735, 10 A.M.–5:30 P.M. Tues.–Fri.), which houses the **Athabasca Archives,** a comprehensive collection of photographs and newspapers.

Muskeg Creek Park, on the west side of town, offers hiking trails and good fishing during spring. The creek flows through a heavily forested ravine into a floodplain, then drains into the Athabasca River. Wildlife abounds, berry picking is good in late summer, and cross-country skiing trails are laid in winter. Access to the park is from the elementary school on 48th Avenue.

On the west side of town, **Athabasca University** (780/675-6111, www.athabascau.ca) has a 12,000-square-meter (130,000-square-foot) facility on a 180-hectare (450-acre) site. It has a full-time staff of 1,200; a choice of 700 programs at all levels, including master's; a library with 100,000 books; an extensive art collection; a fitness facility; and an annual budget exceeding $110 million—but there's not a single student in sight. That's because it's a correspondence university, one of the largest in North America and open to students regardless of their geographical location or previous academic levels. The 37,000 enrolled students work from home, communicating with their tutors via email, phone, fax, and snail mail.

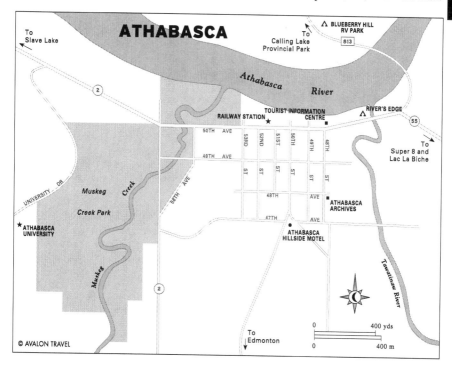

NORTHERN ALBERTA

© ANDREW HEMPSTEAD

Head to this rail carriage in Athabasca for information on the area.

The campus is open to the public and has some unique artworks commissioned especially for the building.

Accommodations

Several motels are on Highway 2 south of town, including **Athabasca Hillside Motel** (4804 46th Ave., 780/675-5111 or 888/675-8900, www.athabascahillsidemotel.net, $65–90 s, $75–95 d), with kitchenettes in each of the 17 rooms. Much nicer is the **Super 8** (4820 Wood Heights Rd., 780/675-8888 or 800/800-8000, www.super8.com, $129 s or d), to the east of town. It's a larger, modern hotel with spacious rooms, a business center, free breakfast, and an adjacent A&W restaurant. **River's Edge Campground** (50th Ave., May–Aug., unserviced sites $15, powered sites $20) sits on the edge of downtown where the Tawatinaw River drains into the much-wider Athabasca River. Amenities are limited to a small bathroom complex with coin showers. Most RVers head north across the river to **Blueberry Hill RV Park** (Hwy. 813, 780/675-3733 or 800/859-

9452, www.blueberryhillrvpark.ca, May–Oct., tenting $22, hookups $29), which has pull-through sites, modern washrooms, a laundry, a playground, and free firewood. It's also adjacent to an excellent golf course.

Information

The tourist information center (50th Ave., 780/675-9297, 10 a.m.–8 p.m. daily late May–early Sept.) is in an orange Canadian National Railway caboose along the riverfront.

Amber Valley

This small hamlet just east of Athabasca was first settled in 1910 by 200 blacks from Oklahoma. They moved from their homeland to escape racial persecution, led north by 22-year-old Jefferson Davis Edwards. The prejudice continued in Alberta, with locals suggesting they should head south because the climate wouldn't suit them. Despite the hard times, the community thrived and remained virtually all black. Since World War II, the population has declined, and today only a few black families remain.

ATHABASCA TO SLAVE LAKE

From Athabasca, Highway 2 heads northwest to Slave Lake, passing many summer communities along the shores of **Baptiste** and **Island Lakes,** both of which have good fishing for northern pike; their campgrounds are inexpensive. This section of the highway is known as the **Northern Woods and Water Route.** Just before **Hondo,** the route intersects Highway 44, which heads south 106 kilometers (66 miles) to Westlock and Highway 18. At Hondo, 72 kilometers (45 miles) from Athabasca, Highway 2A leads to **Fawcett Lake,** known for its good walleye fishing. At the lake are two campgrounds, cabins, and boat rentals.

SLAVE LAKE

The town of Slave Lake (pop. 6,700) is located on the southeastern shore of **Lesser Slave Lake,** 250 kilometers (155 miles) northwest of Edmonton. It began as an important staging point for steamboat freight and passengers heading for the Peace River Country and Yukon goldfields. The arrival of a rail line in 1914 meant a boom time for the fledgling community and the beginning of a lumber industry that continues today. In 1935, disastrous floods destroyed many of the buildings on the main street. Following that debacle, the town was relocated 3.5 kilometers (2.1 miles) to the south. Only a few foundations remain of the original settlement. Today the town has little to interest visitors, but Lesser Slave Lake has some of the best fishing in the province, with northern pike to nine kilograms (20 pounds), walleye to four kilograms (nine pounds), whitefish to 2.5 kilograms (5.5 pounds), and yellow perch to one kilogram (2.2 pounds)—enough to make any self-respecting fisherman quit his job, pack the rod and reel, and head north.

◖ Lesser Slave Lake Provincial Park

At this 7,290-hectare (18,000-acre) park north of town, you'll find a campground, long sandy beaches, unique sand dunes, and wetland and boreal forest habitats supporting diverse wildlife. Offshore is **Dog Island,** the lake's only island, home to a pair of bald eagles, pelicans, and other shorebirds. North of the Lesser Slave River are many access roads leading to **Devonshire Beach,** a seven-kilometer (4.3-mile) stretch of sandy beach popular for sunbathing and swimming. The sunsets from this beach are spectacular (at the north end is a viewing platform). The **North Shore,** to the north of Devonshire Beach, has a picnic area and provides access to the 23-kilometer (14.2-mile) **Freighter Lakeshore Trail,** which

ISN'T SLAVE LAKE IN THE ARCTIC?

Well, no, but an explanation is in order. Lesser Slave Lake is one of *two* Slave Lakes in northwestern Canada. Both lakes are at the same longitude, but they're about 600 kilometers (370 miles) apart as the crow flies. The bigger one – the one that many people *think* is in the Arctic – is north of Alberta in the Northwest Territories (but still south of the Arctic Circle). The smaller, more southerly of the two is here in northern Alberta. Both are named after the Slavey Indians who traveled south up the Athabasca River from the big Slave Lake to the smaller Slave Lake on hunting and fishing expeditions. In early writings, and on maps, both lakes were denoted as Slave Lake. This led to confusion, especially because both were in what was then the Northwest Territories. To remedy the problem, the larger, northern body of water was renamed Great Slave Lake, and its Albertan counterpart, Lesser Slave Lake. Lesser Slave Lake is the third-largest lake in Alberta (only lakes Athabasca and Claire are larger) and the largest accessible by road. It is 90 kilometers (56 miles) long, 20 kilometers (12.5 miles) wide, has an area of 1,150 square kilometers (440 square miles), and is relatively shallow, especially along the south shore, where deltas have formed from the many northward-flowing Swan Hills watersheds.

runs the entire length of the park. North Shore beaches are nonexistent, but a gravel road heading back toward Devonshire leads to a quiet one. At the north end of the park, a steep eight-kilometer (five-mile) road leads through a dense forest of lodgepole pine to the plateaulike summit of 1,030-meter (3,380-foot) Marten Mountain. The views are spectacular from this vantage point 500 meters (1,640 feet) above the lake. A 2.8-kilometer (1.7-mile) trail from the summit winds through an old-growth forest of balsam fir that has escaped major fires. The trail ends up at **Lily Lake,** a small, secluded lake (stocked with rainbow trout) from where Lily Creek flows into Lesser Slave Lake.

WHY ARE SO MANY THINGS NAMED "SAWRIDGE"?

The original settlement on Lesser Slave Lake was named Sawridge, for the jagged range of hills to the north. Many prominent residents didn't like the name, so in 1922, they changed it to Slave Lake, but the original name lives on. Today it's the name of the local Indian band and a creek flowing through town, and many local businesses use the name as well.

Fishing

Although fishing from the lake's edge and in nearby rivers can be productive, the big ones are hooked out on the lake, where pike grow to nine kilograms (20 pounds) and walleye to four kilograms (nine pounds). Ask at the information center for fishing guides and rental outlets. For a small motorboat, expect to pay $25 per hour, $60 half day, or $120 full day.

Pilots at **Canwest Air** (780/849-5353), based at the airport in town, will fly you to their favorite fishing lakes. Orloff Lake is a half hour to the east and has a campsite (flight is $425 for up to five people), and God's Lake is one hour north (flight is $675). If the pilot knows that the fishing is good, he won't charge you for the time spent on the ground between landing and takeoff (ground time).

Accommodations and Camping

The **Highway Motor Inn,** on Highway 2 by the tourist information center (600 14th Ave. SW, 780/849-2400 or 888/848-2400), has 75 basic rooms for $65 s, $75 d. The **Sawridge Inn and Conference Centre** (1200 Main St. S., 780/849-4101 or 800/661-6657, www. sawridge.com, $119 s, $129 d) is set on a large chunk of land at the entrance to town. It attracts a mix of business and highway travelers with the amenities of a full-service hotel and in-house dining options that include an English-style pub. The Business Class rooms

are decidedly bigger than the standard rooms and come with Internet access and bathrobes for just $10 extra.

Lesser Slave Lake Provincial Park's **Marten River Campground** (6 km/3.7 miles north of town, 780/849-7100, May–Oct., unserviced sites $20, powered sites $26) has coin-operated showers, a beach, and a summer interpretive program.

Food

The **Hearthstone Grille,** in the Sawridge Inn (1200 Main St. S., 780/849-4101), is a casual dining room with bright decor and a relaxed atmosphere. It offers a good breakfast buffet with a wide selection of dishes ($10.95). The **Sawridge Truckstop** (on the corner of Hwy. 88 and Caribou Trail NE, 780/849-4030) is just that—a truck stop with vinyl seats, hearty meals, inexpensive prices, and very busy waitresses. It's open 24 hours.

Information

The tourist information center (off Hwy. 2, west of Main St., 780/849-4611, www. slavelake.com) is open 10 A.M.–7 P.M. daily May–August.

Bicentennial Highway

This 430-kilometer (270-mile) road (also known as Highway 88) connects Slave Lake with Fort Vermilion to the north and is an excellent alternative to the Mackenzie Highway for those traveling in that direction. It was renamed and renumbered to commemorate the bicentenary of Fort Vermilion in 1988. Services (gas, rooms, and restaurant) are available at the only community along the road, **Red Earth Creek**—a semipermanent oil-fields town 130 kilometers (81 miles) north of Slave Lake. From there, Highway 686 heads east to **Peerless** and **Trout Lakes,** named for the excellent fishing, and west to the town of Peace River.

At Red Earth Creek, the Bicentennial Highway becomes a gravel road and parallels the Loon and Wabasca Rivers, following the eastern flanks of the **Buffalo Head Hills.** Seventy kilometers (43 miles) from Fort Vermilion, a turnoff to the west leads to **Wadlin Lake,** home to one of Alberta's four colonies of white pelicans. They nest on an island during summer, migrating south to the Gulf of Mexico each winter. The island is a Prohibited Access Wildlife Area, and the birds should not be disturbed during the breeding season because they are prone to abandoning their nests if approached. The lake has good fishing for northern pike and whitefish, and a primitive campground with sites for $12 a night.

TO THE PEACE RIVER

From Slave Lake, Highway 2 westbound follows the southern shore of Lesser Slave Lake to High Prairie. At **Kinuso** a small museum (780/775-3774, 10 A.M.–4 P.M. Mon.–Fri. May–Aug., donation) centers around a stuffed grizzly bear that stands over 2.5 meters (eight feet) tall. A little farther along the highway, a nine-kilometer (5.6-mile) gravel road leads north to Lesser Slave Lake and **C Spruce Point Park** (780/775-2117, www.sprucepoint-park.ca, mid-May–mid-Sept., $21–28), which bustles with families and fishermen throughout summer. From the main camping area, a wide grassed area leads down to a lakefront beach and a marina with boat and canoe rentals and a fish-cleaning shed. Other park amenities include a general store (stocked with lots of fishing tackle), horseshoe pits, hiking trails, and showers.

Grouard and Vicinity

A town of 400 on Buffalo Bay near the west end of Lesser Slave Lake, Grouard grew up around the St. Bernard Mission, founded in 1884 by Father Emile Grouard. The town was destined to become the center of the north. It had a few thousand people and a rail line on the way, when, because of an unfortunate set of circumstances, everything changed. A sample of water from a nearby lake was sent to the railway headquarters to ensure that it was fit for the steam engines. Along the way it was either dropped, lost, or emptied and replaced by a sample of water from muskeg wetland. The new sample was tested and found to be of poor quality. The proposed route for the railway changed, and the once-thriving town collapsed.

On the grounds of Northern Lakes College, the **Native Cultural Arts Museum** (780/751-3306, 10 A.M.–4 P.M. Tues.–Fri., 10 A.M.–6 P.M. Sat. May–Sept., donation) is dedicated to promoting a better understanding of North American native cultures through exhibition of native arts and crafts as well as the outdoor re-creation of a native village.

Hilliard's Bay Provincial Park is 13 kilometers (eight miles) east of Grouard on the northwest shore of Lesser Slave Lake. It is a 2,330-hectare (5,800-acre) park with mixed woods, two sandy beaches, and a one-kilometer (0.6-mile) spit framed by a stand of gnarled paper birches. The **Boreal Forest Interpretive Trail** meanders through a forest habitat, where many species of mammals are present—look for tracks along the top of the ridges at the east end of the park. The park campground (780/849-7124, May–early Oct., unserviced sites $20, powered sites $26) has showers, kitchen shelters, and firewood.

Like Spruce Point Park near Kinuso, **Shaw's Point Lakeside Resort** (780/751-3900, www. shawspointresort.com, Apr.–Oct., camping $28–37, cabins $125–145 s or d) is a full-service campground catering mostly to families and fishing enthusiasts. Facilities include two marinas, pontoon boat rentals (from $25 per hour), a par-3 golf course, a restaurant

(8 A.M.–10 P.M. daily), a general store, show-ers, wireless Internet, and a laundry room. Access is from the road leading into Hillard's Bay Provincial Park. On the second week-end of August, Shaw's Point hosts the **Golden Walleye Classic** (www.goldenwalleyeclassic. com), North America's richest catch-and-re-lease walleye tournament, with over $100,000 in cash up for grabs. Walleye fishing is not the world's most exciting spectator sport, but am-ateur anglers are welcome to enter for $1,000 per boat.

Winagami Lake Provincial Park

Winagami Lake, north of High Prairie on Highway 749, is ringed by a mix of paper birch, aspen, balsam fir, and poplar trees. The park is on the lake's eastern shore and is an excel-lent place for bird-watching; two platforms have been built for this purpose (the best time of year is May–June). The day-use area has been planted with ornamental shrubs, and a short hiking trail leads along the lakeshore to a bird-watching platform. The campground (780/523-0041, May–mid-Oct., unserviced sites $20, powered sites $25) has pit toilets, firewood, and kitchen shelters.

Winagami Wildland Park, along the north-eastern arm of the lake (turn off 9 km/5.6 miles south of McLennan), is also good for bird-watching. It's undeveloped except for a few short trails.

McLennan

Known as the Bird Capital of Canada, this town of 1,000 is on **Kimiwan Lake** at the con-fluence of three major bird migration paths—the Mississippi, Pacific, and Central. An estimated 27,000 shorebirds and 250,000 wa-terfowl reside or pass through here; more than 200 different species are sighted annually. An excellent interpretive center (780/324-2004, 10 A.M.–7 P.M. daily May–Sept.) overlooking the lake has a display on migration patterns, computers loaded with information on local species, checklists, and binoculars for loan. From the center, a boardwalk leads through a wetland area to a gazebo and a bird blind.

Panels along the boardwalk provide pic-tures and descriptions of commonly sighted species.

Continuing West

The small hamlet of **Donnelly,** 14 kilometers (8.7 miles) west of McLennan, is best known for the annual **Smoky River Agricultural Fair** (780/925-3835), held the second weekend of August. The fair features home cooking, a pa-rade, a petting zoo, demonstrations of country skills, a country-style beauty contest (the best-looking tractor wins), and the highlight of the weekend—the Antique Tractor Pull.

From west of Donnelly, Highway 2 heads north 63 kilometers (39 miles) to the town of Peace River. Highway 49 continues west to Spirit River and the turnoff to Grande Prairie. The first town along this route is **Falher,** known as the Honey Capital of Canada. One million bees in 48,000 hives produce 4.5 mil-lion kilograms (10 million pounds) of honey annually. Naturally, this industry has created a need for the town to construct the world's largest honeybee, which towers above a small park on Third Avenue (the main drag through town). At the east end of town are two strange-smelling alfalfa-processing plants. The alfalfa is dehydrated and pressed into pellets—more than 50,000 tons annually. You can watch all the action from the highway.

HIGHWAY 18 WEST

Seventy-three kilometers (45 miles) north of Edmonton on Highway 2, Highway 18 heads west through some of Canada's most produc-tive mixed farming land. Major crops include wheat, barley, oats, canola, and hay. Livestock operations include cattle, hogs, poultry, dairy cows, and sheep; the area is home to several large feedlots and Alberta's two largest live-stock auctions. At the junction of Highways 2 and 18, a gravel road leads north to **Nilsson Bros. Inc.** (780/348-5893, www.nbinc.com), Canada's largest cattle auction market. Live auctions are held in summer every Tuesday morning. Buyers are from throughout North America, but anyone is welcome to attend. The auctioneer is lightning fast—Alberta's best beef cattle are sold hundreds at a time by gross weight. The facility is open every day; ask to have a look around. The staff restaurant, open for an hour at lunchtime, serves hearty meat-and-potato meals for a reasonable price. Just don't ask for lamb.

Highway 44 North

Highway 44 spurs north from Highway 18 at **Westlock,** an agricultural service center 11 kilometers (6.8 miles) west of Highway 2. It has the small **Westlock Pionner Museum** (10216 100th St., 780/349-4849, 10 A.M.–5 P.M. daily late May–Aug., adult $3, child $1.50), which is also the local information center, filled with pioneer artifacts including guns, lamps, and a fire engine.

From Westlock, it is 106 kilometers (66 miles) north along Highway 44 to Hondo, halfway between Athabasca and Slave Lake. Along the way are two worthwhile detours. **Long Island Lake Municipal Park** (go 22 km/13.6 miles north from Westlock, then turn right at Dapp Corner and follow the signs) is a recreation area with fishing, swimming, canoeing, and camping (May–Sept., $18). Farther north, near the hamlet of Fawcett, is a turn-off to 2,068-hectare (5,150-acre) **Cross Lake Provincial Park.** Deer and moose are common here, and in late summer black bears often feed among the berry patches. A number of trails crisscross the park, some leading to the lake edge. The shallow lake is good for swimming, canoeing, and fishing for northern pike. The campground (780/675-8213, May–mid-Oct., unserviced sites $20, powered sites $26) has pit toilets, firewood, kitchen shelters, coin-operated showers, and a concession.

Barrhead and Vicinity

Continuing west on Highway 18 takes you to Barrhead, an agriculture and lumber town of 4,200 located 1.5 hours northwest of Edmonton. **Barrhead Centennial Museum** (along Hwy. 33 at 57th Ave., 780/674-5203, 10 A.M.–5 P.M. Tues.–Sat., 1–5 P.M. Sun. mid-May–Aug., adult $2), with displays depicting

© ANDREW HEMPSTEAD

This blue heron welcomes visitors to Barrhead.

the town's agricultural past, is north of downtown. The town's symbol is the great blue heron; you can see a model of one at the top end of 50th Street, or head out to Thunder Lake Provincial Park for the chance to see a real one. The biggest event of the year is the **Wildrose Rodeo Association Finals** (www.wrarodeo.com), on the third weekend of September.

An interesting loop drive from Barrhead is to take Highway 769 north to **Neerlandia** (settled by the Dutch in 1912 and named after their homeland), the small hamlet of **Vega,** and the Athabasca River. The river crossing is on the **Klondike Ferry,** one of the province's few remaining ferries. The next community along this route is **Fort Assiniboine,** which was a vital link in the Hudson's Bay Company chain of fur-trading posts. The original fort was built in 1824, making it one of the oldest settlements in Alberta. Although furs were traded at the fort, its main role was as a transportation link across the then-uncharted wilderness. The original is long gone, but a reconstruction is in the center of town (noon–5 P.M. daily in summer).

From Fort Assiniboine, it is 38 kilometers (24 miles) southeast back to Barrhead, completing the loop, or 62 kilometers (38 miles) northwest to Swan Hills.

Thunder Lake Provincial Park

Colonies of great blue herons reside at this 208-hectare (514-acre) park, 21 kilometers (13 miles) west of Barrhead on Highway 18. The park is on the northeast shore of shallow Thunder Lake, set among stands of aspen and balsam fir. Bird-watching, especially for waterfowl, is excellent; look for herons on the islands in the quiet northwest corner of the lake. Grebes and black terns are also common. The lake's water level is artificially controlled to prevent flooding of cottages and beaches. This control results in poor fishing, although the lake is stocked annually with northern pike and perch. Three short hiking trails begin from the day-use area, including one along the lakeshore that links to three other trails originating from the campground. The campground (780/674-4051, mid-Apr.–mid-Oct., $23–28) is beside the beach. It has pit toilets, coin-operated showers, a concession, firewood, kitchen shelters, and canoe rentals.

SWAN HILLS

The town of Swan Hills (pop. 1,800) is in the hills of the same name, 100 kilometers (62 miles) northwest of Barrhead. The hills were named, according to Indian legend, for giant swans that nested in a nearby river estuary. It's in the center of a region rich in oil and gas but is best known economically for the **Swan Hills Treatment Centre,** one of the world's most modern special-waste treatment plants, which treats material that cannot be disposed of in a landfill, incinerator, or sewage system. Corrosive, combustible, and environmentally unfriendly materials such as lead, mercury, and pesticides are broken down into nontoxic compounds using a process of thermal oxidization and then either burned off or safely stored. Up to 45,000 tons of waste can be treated annually.

The surrounding hills are wetter than the Canadian Rockies foothills, creating a unique environment of rainforest, boreal, and subarctic zones. The best place to observe this blend is at **Goose Mountain Ecological Reserve,** 24 kilometers (15 miles) west of town. Hiking and fishing are popular activities throughout the hills; the easiest area to access is **Krause Lake Recreation Area,** south of town. Old logging roads crisscross the entire region, making exploration easy with a full tank of gas and a map from the local information center. The hills provide refuge for the **Swan Hills grizzly bear,** a subspecies of the now-extinct plains grizzly and the only grizzly east of the Rocky Mountains.

The **Grizzly Trail** (Highway 33), linking Barrhead and Swan Hills, offers two interesting stops along its route. **Trapper Lea's Cabin** is 30 kilometers (19 miles) southeast of Swan Hills. It consists of two buildings constructed on the trapline of the Wolf King of Alberta, the man who trapped the most wolves in the province during the early 1940s. Five kilometers (3.1 miles) farther south is a highway rest area from where a three-kilometer (1.9-mile) trail leads to the **geographic center of Alberta.** Follow the brown and yellow signs along an old seismic road to the center, indicated by an orange marker.

Accommodations and Camping

Swan Hills has several roadside motels, but each is usually full with work crews. Try the **Derrick Motor Inn** (in the plaza, 780/333-4405, $75 s, $85 d), although rooms are older and overpriced. Instead of staying at the unappealing campground in town, head 30 kilometers (19 miles) southeast to **Trapper Lea's Recreation Area** (May–Oct., $10) or 16 kilometers (10 miles) south to **Freeman River Recreation Area** (May–mid-Oct., $10).

Carson-Pegasus Provincial Park

This 1,178-hectare (2,900-acre) park is on the southern edge of the Swan Hills, 49 kilometers (30 miles) south of the town of Swan Hills and 30 kilometers (19 miles) north of Whitecourt. Because of its location in a transition zone, it contains forest typical of both the foothills (lodgepole pine and spruce) and the boreal forest (aspen, poplar, birch, and fir). More than 40 species of mammals have been recorded here, including deer, moose, and black bear. The epicenter of the park is McLeod Lake, where the fishing is excellent for rainbow trout (stocked annually) and the day-use area offers inexpensive canoe, rowboat, and motorboat rentals and a sandy beach. Northern pike, perch, and whitefish are caught in Little McLeod Lake. The general store (9 A.M.–9 P.M. daily in summer) sells groceries, fishing tackle, bait, and hot food, and has a laundry room. The campground (780/778-2664, www.carsonpegasus.com, $22–28, firewood $7) has over 180 sites, flush toilets, showers, kitchen shelters, and an interpretive theater.

WHITECOURT

Whitecourt (pop. 9,000) sits at the confluence of the Athabasca, McLeod, and Sakwatamau Rivers on Highway 43, 177 kilometers (110 miles) northwest of Edmonton and 341 kilometers (212 miles) southeast of Grande Prairie. Highway 32 also passes through town; Swan Hills is 74 kilometers (46 miles) north, and the Yellowhead Highway is 72 kilometers (45 miles) south. If you're coming in from the southeast, you'll pass a strip of motels and restaurants before descending to the Athabasca River and the older part of town, off to the right. Many of Whitecourt's earliest settlers were Yukon-bound in search of gold when they reached this lushly forested region and decided to settle here instead. To them, the area held plenty of opportunities that wouldn't require an arduous trek to the Klondike. When the railroad arrived, so did many more homesteaders. They took to cutting down trees to sell for firewood and railroad ties. Thus began Whitecourt's lumber industry; today the town is the Forest Centre of Alberta.

Sights

The two-story **Forest Interpretive Centre** (on the south side of town, 780/778-2214, 9 A.M.–6 P.M. daily July–Aug., 9 A.M.–6 P.M.

Mon.–Fri. the rest of the year, free) is dedicated to Alberta's forest industry. Displays re-create a forest environment and a logging camp, and a series of hands-on, interactive exhibits describe every aspect of the industry. The center also holds the town's information center (780/778-5363). Industrial tours are run by the interpretive center Monday–Friday in summer. Each of the four tours is to a forestry-related industry—a pulp mill, a newsprint plant, a sawmill, and a medium-density fiberboard plant. The **E. S. Huestis Demonstration Forest,** five kilometers (3.1 miles) north of Highway 43 on Highway 32, contains several stages of forest development. A seven-kilometer (4.3-mile) road leads through various ecosystems, including an old-growth coniferous forest and a deciduous forest, and past aspen and spruce cut blocks, a beaver dam, and an exotic plantation.

Accommodations and Camping

Most of Whitecourt's dozen motels are on Highway 43 as it enters town from the southeast. The best of these, **Green Gables Inn** (3527 Caxton St., 780/778-4537 or 888/779-4537, www.greengablesinn.ca, $104 s, $109 d), has large, surprisingly nice rooms, wireless Internet, an exercise room, and a restaurant (where guests enjoy complimentary breakfast).

The **Lions Club Campground** (mid-Apr.–mid-Oct., tent sites $20, RVs $24–28), at the south end of the service strip, is set in a heavily forested area and has a laundry and showers. A nicer option is the campground at **Carson-Pegasus Provincial Park,** 30 kilometers (19 miles) north of town on Highway 32.

HIGHWAY 43 WEST

From Whitecourt, Highway 43 continues northeast to **Fox Creek,** a small town surrounded by a wilderness where wildlife is abundant and the fishing legendary. If you don't believe the local fishing stories, head to the Home Hardware Store to see a 12-kilogram (26-pound) northern pike caught in a nearby lake. **Smoke** and **Iosegun Lakes** are two of the most accessible and offer excellent fishing for northern pike, walleye, perch, and white-fish. Both lakes have primitive camping.

Moose are abundant between Fox Creek and **Little Smoky,** 47 kilometers (26 miles) north-west, from where gravel roads lead to small lakes. This area is not noted for fossils, but a few years back a mammoth tusk was found in Waskahigan River, west of Little Smoky.

Valleyview

Valleyview (pop. 2,000) is an agricultural and oil and gas center that also serves travelers who pass through heading north to the Northwest Territories and west to Alaska. It is also one of the largest towns in Alberta without a pioneer museum.

The town's three motels fill up each night with road-weary travelers. The **Horizon Motel** (780/524-3904 or 888/909-3908) has large rooms in an older wing ($75 s, $85 d), but make sure to request those in the newer wing, which are $20 extra. Spend the night with Alaska-bound campers at **Sherk's RV Park** (south side of town, 780/524-4949, May–Sept., $28), a full-service campground.

Valleyview Tourist Information Centre (3 km/1.9 miles south of town, 780/524-2410) is open 8 A.M.–8 P.M. daily mid-May–September.

Sturgeon Lake

Sturgeon Lake, west of Valleyview, is known for its excellent northern pike, perch, and walleye fishing and two interesting provincial parks. **Williamson Provincial Park** may be only 17 hectares (42 acres), but it has a sandy beach, good swimming, and a campground (780/538-5350, mid-May–mid-Oct., unserviced sites $20, powered sites $26). Protecting a much larger chunk of forested lakeshore is 3,100-hectare (7,660-acre) **Young's Point Provincial Park.** Here you'll find good bird-watching for forest birds and waterfowl, and productive fishing among the dense aquatic growth close to the shore. Much of the park is forested with a blend of aspen, white spruce, and lodgepole pine. Porcupine, deer, and coyote wander the woods here, and if you're lucky, you might see red fox, lynx, and black bear. Hiking trails begin at the day-use area and lead along the lake and to an active beaver pond. The campground (780/538-5350, unserviced sites $20, powered sites $25) has flush toilets and showers, and is near a sandy beach.

West of Edmonton

From the provincial capital, the Yellowhead Highway (Highway 16) heads west through a region of aspen parkland and scattered lakes to the Canadian Rockies foothills and the border of Jasper National Park. The region's other main thoroughfare, Highway 40, spurs north off the Yellowhead Highway to Grande Cache and Willmore Wilderness Park. An area of frenzied oil activity during the early 1970s, the region west of Edmonton is the center for a large petroleum industry, as well as for farming, coal mining, forestry, and the production of electricity. The major towns are Edson and Hinton, both on the Yellowhead Highway.

FROM EDMONTON TOWARD HINTON

Long after leaving Edmonton's city limits, the Yellowhead Highway is lined with motels, industrial parks, and housing estates. The towns of Spruce Grove and Stony Plain flash by, and farming begins to dominate the landscape.

Wabamun and Nearby Lakes

Wabamun is the name of a town, lake, and provincial park 32 kilometers (20 miles) west of Stony Plain. The skyline around Wabamun Lake is dominated by high-voltage power lines coming from the three coal-fired generating plants that supply more than two-thirds

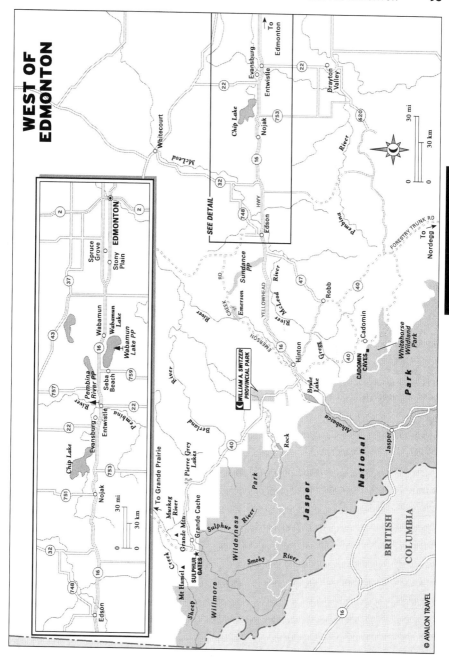

NORTHERN ALBERTA

© AVALON TRAVEL

of Alberta's electrical requirements. Fuel for the plants is supplied by nearby mining operations—the largest coal extraction sites in Canada.

Wabamun Lake Provincial Park is on sparkling blue Moonlight Bay at the lake's eastern end. The fishing is good for northern pike (especially in fall), a man-made beach is the perfect spot for a swim, and the hiking trail is a good spot for wildlife viewing. Two geothermal outlets create a perfect environment for waterfowl in winter; expect to see up to 40 species at each site. The easiest outlet to get to is at the end of the wharf. The park campground (780/892-2702, mid-May–early Oct., unserviced sites $20, powered sites $25) has 276 sites (including 111 powered sites), but because of its proximity to Edmonton is very busy on weekends. Facilities include coin-operated showers, firewood, kitchen shelters, and a concession.

Pembina River Provincial Park and Vicinity

The Pembina River Valley is the first true wilderness area west of Edmonton. The small towns of Entwistle and Evansburg straddle either side of the valley where the park lies. The only structures you'll see in this 167-hectare (413-acre) park are an old single-lane road bridge and the concrete foundations of what once was a railroad trestle. White spruce and aspen blanket the park and provide a habitat for many mammals, including beavers, mule deer, white-tailed deer, and moose. Fishing in the river is particularly good for northern pike and walleye, and those who don't fish might appreciate the deep swimming hole behind a weir, or the hiking trails in the northern part of the park. On the eastern side of the river, the campground (780/727-3643, mid-May–Oct., unserviced sites $20, powered sites $26) has flush toilets, kitchen shelters, showers, an interpretive program, and firewood.

Highway 16 bypasses **Entwistle,** but the town's main street is worth a look for its historic buildings. Out on the highway are all the services you'll need: motels (from $60 s, $70 d), restaurants, gas, and, of course, minigolf.

Continuing west on Highway 16 toward Edson, you'll pass **Chip Lake,** interesting primarily for the scatological story behind its name. It used to be called Buffalo Chip Lake, but the name was shortened for aesthetic reasons.

Edson

The site of today's town of Edson was once the starting point of a trail early settlers used to access the Peace River Valley to the north. Later, the site was picked as a divisional point of the Grand Trunk Pacific Railway, and the town sprang up around it. Today this town of 8,100, 199 kilometers (124 miles) west of Edmonton, relies on natural-resource-based industries such as forestry and oil and gas to fuel its economy.

Most motels are along the main highway through town—locally known as 2nd Avenue (heading east) and 4th Avenue (heading west). **Odyssey Inn** (5601 2nd Ave., 780/723-5505, $85 s, $95 d) offers acceptable rooms. The **Sundowner Inn** (5150 2nd Ave., 780/723-5591 or 877/723-5591, $99 s, $109 d) has the basics and a few bonuses, too—an indoor pool and a recreation room with a fireplace and pool table.

Lions Park Campground (east end of town, 780/723-3169, May–Sept., unserviced sites $18, powered sites $21) has 48 treed sites far enough from the highway to be relatively quiet. Facilities include extra-hot (and fast) showers and plenty of free firewood, which is just as well because you need a bonfire to cook anything on the oversized fire rings.

Ernie O's (4340 2nd Ave., 780/723-3600, $10–22) is one of the best places in town to eat breakfast ($7–11). Nightly specials are $15, and all mains come with a salad bar. **Mountain Pizza & Steakhouse** (5102 4th Ave., 780/723-3900) is a pizza joint where the food and prices are excellent. The Mountain Extra Special Pizza ($22) is worth the extra bucks, or if it's Saturday, the prime rib special is an easy choice.

The tourist information center is in the RCMP Centennial Park (3rd Ave., 780/723-4918, www.townofedson.ca, 8 A.M.–8 P.M. Mon.–Fri. and 9 A.M.–8 P.M. Sat.–Sun. mid-

May–Aug., 8 A.M.–4 P.M. weekdays only the rest of the year).

Sundance Provincial Park

As an alternative to continuing west along Highway 16 from Edson to Hinton, consider the **Emerson Creek Road,** which links the two towns, running north of and parallel to Highway 16. The road passes through the 3,712-hectare (9,170-acre) Sundance Provincial Park, protecting a variety of interesting geological features and the picturesque Emerson Lakes. (Emerson Creek Road is maintained primarily as a logging road, so drive with care and yield to trucks—yellow signs along the road are not kilometer markers.) From Edson, take 51st Street north from Highway 16 for 32 kilometers (20 miles), turning left (to the west) at the Silver Summit ski area sign; this is Emerson Creek Road, and from this point it's 83 kilometers (52 miles) to Hinton.

The two picturesque Emerson Lakes, between signs 53 and 52, were formed as the sheet of ice from the last ice age receded. A 5.7-kilometer (3.5-mile) trail winds around the lakes to an old trapper's cabin and past some active beaver dams; allow 90 minutes to complete the entire loop. The lakes are stocked with brook trout and Sundance Creek with rainbow and brown trout. A small campground (May–Sept., $10) at the lakes has sites with no facilities but free firewood. In the west of the park, between signs 18 and 19, a short trail follows **Canyon Creek** to a point where it cascades dramatically into a series of canyons.

If you're traveling west to east, the access point in Hinton is a little more difficult to find: take Switzer Drive south from Highway 16 and loop back under Highway 16, then continue for four kilometers (2.5 miles). Turn left (north) at Weldwood Bridge Road. Continue down to a bridge over the Athabasca River and follow this road until Emerson Creek Road is signed to the right.

HINTON

On the south bank of the Athabasca River and surrounded in total wilderness, this town

of 9,500, 287 kilometers (178 miles) west of Edmonton, makes an ideal base for a couple of days' exploration. It's also only 75 kilometers (47 miles) from Jasper, but before speeding off to the famous mountain parks, take time out to explore Hinton's immediate vicinity. To the south are well-maintained roads leading into the historic Coal Branch; to the north are lakes, streams, canyons, hoodoos, and sand dunes. The town has some interesting sights, and the motels and restaurants have prices you'll appreciate after spending time in Jasper.

Hinton began as a coal-mining and forestry town. These industries still play a major role in the town's economy, although the town now also benefits from being an important service stop along the Yellowhead Highway.

Don't be put off by the unappealing location of the **Natural Resource Interpretive Park,** behind the Canadian Tire store on the west side of town—much of the park is out of sight in the valley below. Up top are a lookout, a 154-ton dump truck, and panels describing local industry, while a trail leads down to a small arboretum and through an

Natural Resource Interpretive Park, Hinton

© ANDREW HEMPSTEAD

NORTHERN ALBERTA

area of wetlands. On the campus of the **Hinton Training Centre** (1176 Switzer Dr., 780/865-8200, 8:30 A.M.–4:30 P.M. Mon.–Fri.) you'll find a small museum dedicated to the history of forestry, including a display on wildfire management. Adjacent is a 1922 ranger cabin. The museum is also the starting point for the **Interpretive Nature Trail**—a 1.6-kilometer (one-mile) path that winds around the perimeter of the school, passing various forest environments, Edna the erratic (a huge boulder carried far from its source during the last ice age), and a viewpoint with magnificent views of the Athabasca River Valley and Canadian Rockies.

Accommodations and Camping

The strip of motels, hotels, restaurants, fast-food places, and gas stations along Highway 16 reflects the importance of Hinton as a service center, but I recommend passing up the regular motels and staying out of town.

Halfway between Hinton and Jasper, **C Overlander Mountain Lodge** (780/866-2330 or 877/866-2330, www.overlander-mountainlodge.com, $159–219 s or d) has an inviting wilderness setting and energetic hosts with plenty of suggestions to keep you busy throughout the day. Choose from regular guest rooms in various styles (the Miette Rooms have a particularly appealing decor), cozy cabins, or a large three-bedroom log chalet. Mountain charm continues through to the dining room, where Canadian specialties anchor a seasonal menu.

If it's just a bed for the night you're after, it's hard to go past the **Best Canadian Motor Inn** (386 Smith St., 780/865-5099 or 888/700-2264, www.bestcdn.com, $99 s or d, kitchenette $115), along the main commercial strip. It offers 40 clean, medium-size rooms decorated in an unfussy alpine style. Amenities in each include in-room coffee and Internet access. A light breakfast is included in the rates. **Holiday Inn Hinton** (393 Gregg Ave., 780/865-3321 or 888/465-4329, www.holidayinn.com, from $119 s, $129 d) has everything you'd expect from a Holiday Inn—reliable rooms, a

restaurant, a fitness room, and kid-friendly extras like PlayStation.

The best nearby camping is in **William A. Switzer Provincial Park** toward Grande Cache, which has three campgrounds (Gregg Lake, unserviced sites $20, powered sites $26; Graveyard/Halfway and Cache Campgrounds, $14–17; and Jarvis Lake Campground, $20). For more information on the park, call 780/865-5600; for campsite reservations, call 780/865-5152.

Food

Apart from the fast-food restaurants that line the highway from one end of town to the other, Hinton has little to offer the hungry traveler. The **Husky Restaurant**, as usual, serves filling meals at good prices; open 24 hours. If gas-station dining isn't your style, try the **Greentree Restaurant**, in the Holiday Inn. A continental breakfast is $7.50; the lumberjack breakfast of steak, bacon, eggs, and hotcakes is $14. Lunch is $10–14, and dinner mains start at $15.50. **Tokyo Sushi** (Black Bear Inn, 571 Gregg Ave., 780/865-2120, lunch and dinner Mon.–Sat.) has a modern family-restaurant-style atmosphere and good-value Japanese food. Don't expect anything too adventurous—just tasty, inexpensive favorites like chicken teriyaki ($13) as well as filling sushi combos (from $12).

Information and Services

The **tourist information center** (Gregg Ave., 780/865-2777, 8:30 A.M.–6 P.M. daily in summer, 9 A.M.–4 P.M. Mon.–Fri. the rest of the year) is on the south side of the highway, surrounded by gardens in the middle of the commercial strip. It's impossible to miss. Most of the best this region has to offer lies outside of Hinton, and in this regard, the staff does a wonderful job of supplying information on hiking, fishing, and canoeing opportunities that would otherwise be easy to miss.

The **post office** is on Parks Street.

THE COAL BRANCH

An area of heavily forested foothills south of Hinton has been the scene of feverish coal-mining activity for 90 years. Most of the mines, along with the towns of Mountain Park, Luscar, Leyland, Coal Spur, and Mercoal, have been abandoned. Two mines still operate, and two towns have survived, although the populations of **Cadomin** and **Robb** have dwindled to approximately 100 residents apiece. This area, so rich in history, is also a wilderness offering hiking, fishing, and spectacular views of the Canadian Rockies. The best way to access the region, known as the Coal Branch, is via Highway 40. The active mines are Cardinal River Coal's pit-mining operation and another at Gregg River. A viewpoint overlooks one of the largest pits. Look for bighorn sheep, oblivious to the rumbling trucks below, at natural salt deposits on the cliff above the viewpoint.

From the junction beyond the mines, a spur branches south to Cadomin and Whitehorse Wildland Park; on your return trip, you can take Highway 40 northeast to Highway 47, passing through the coal-mining hamlet of Robb and rejoining Highway 16 just west of Edson. This 250-kilometer (155-mile) loop through the Coal Branch takes at least one day.

Cadomin

This remote little hamlet—once a town of 2,500—is best known as the gateway to Alberta's best known and most accessible caverns, **Cadomin Caves,** which can be seen in the mountain face west of town. Access is along a trail that begins two kilometers (1.2 miles) south of Cadomin, climbing 350 vertical meters (1,150 feet) in three kilometers (1.9 miles) to the mouth of the cave. The caves are closed September–April as they are a hibernaculum for bats. Serious spelunkers can find out more and get a map of the cave system from the information center in Hinton.

Whitehorse Wildland Park

This 17,500-hectare (43,250-acre) area of wilderness lies south and west of Cadomin, adjacent to Jasper National Park. Highway 40 south from Cadomin enters the park after three kilometers (1.9 miles) and crosses Whitehorse

Creek after another two kilometers (1.2 miles). At this bridge is a small campground ($11) nestled below a sheer rock wall. The campground is also the starting point for an overnight backcountry trail over Whitehorse Pass to Miette Hot Springs in Jasper National Park, a total of 40 kilometers (25 miles) one-way. A good turnaround point for a full-day hike is **Whitehorse Falls,** 10 kilometers (6.2 miles) from the trailhead.

Continuing south through the park, Highway 40 climbs above the tree line and passes what's left of **Mountain Park,** once a thriving community of 1,000 connected by rail to Coal Spur to the east. The mine at Mountain Park closed in 1950, and residents dismantled their houses and moved to new locations. Today all that remains is a cemetery, some foundations, and remnants of the narrow-gauge railway.

From here, the road continues climbing to the Cardinal Divide (the division between the Athabasca River System, which flows north, and the North Saskatchewan River System, which flows east), more than 2,000 meters (6,600 feet) above sea level. This magnificent ridge extends as far as the eye can see to the east and west. No trails are marked in this remote corner of the park, but walking through the treeless alpine landscape is possible in either direction.

HIGHWAY 40 TO GRANDE CACHE

Take divided Highway 16 west out of Hinton, and, before you know it, Highway 40 spurs north, passing the following sights and reaching Grande Cache after 142 kilometers (88 miles).

◖ William A. Switzer Provincial Park

This 2,688-hectare (6,640-acre) park, in the foothills 26 kilometers (16 miles) northwest of Hinton on Highway 40, encompasses a series of shallow lakes linked by Jarvis Creek. Most of the park is heavily forested with lodgepole pine, spruce, and aspen. The northern section, however, is more wide open, and elk, moose, and deer can often be seen grazing there. An ill-fated attempt at beaver ranching was made in the 1940s (cement lodges built for the purpose can be seen near Beaver Ranch Campground). Soon after, Entrance Provincial Park was established and renamed Switzer in 1958. The lakes are excellent for canoeing, bird-watching, and wildlife viewing, but fishing is considered average. Highway 40 divides the park roughly in two, with many access points. From the south, the first road loops around the west side of Jarvis Lake, passing a pleasant picnic area and camping before rejoining Highway 40. At the north end of Jarvis Lake is Kelley's Bathtub day-use area, where a short trail leads to a bird blind. The roads leading into the northern section of the park lead past various hiking trails, three more day-use areas, and three campgrounds.

The main campground is on **Gregg Lake.** It offers 164 sites, coin-operated showers, kitchen shelters, an interpretive theater, and winter camping; unserviced sites $20, powered sites $26. In the same vicinity are **Graveyard/ Halfway** and **Cache Campgrounds,** where sites range $14–17 per night. In the south of the park is **Jarvis Lake Campground** ($20). For more information on the park, call 780/865-5600; for campsite reservations, call 780/865-5152.

On to Grande Cache

From William A. Switzer Provincial Park, it is 118 kilometers (73 miles) to Grande Cache.

A 32-kilometer (20-mile) gravel spur to **Rock Lake-Solomon Creek Wildland Provincial Park,** 15 kilometers (9.3 miles) north of Switzer park, makes a tempting detour. Although the park extends from Willmore Wilderness Park in the north to Brûlé Lake in the south, most is a remote, untracked wilderness. The only facilities are at Rock Lake itself. Ever since a Hudson's Bay Company post was established at the lake, the area has drawn hikers and anglers, attracted by mountain scenery, the chance of viewing abundant big game, excellent fishing for huge lake trout, and the remote location. Hiking trails lead around the lake and three kilometers (1.9 miles) to the remote northern reaches of Jasper National Park. Fortunately, you don't have to travel far to appreciate the rugged beauty of the lake and surrounding mountainscapes. The large campground has kitchen shelters, firewood, and pit toilets; sites are $20 per night.

From Rock Lake Road, Highway 40 continues to climb steadily, crossing Pinto Creek and Berland River (small campground), then following Muskeg River for a short while. Continuing north, the road then passes **Pierre Grey Lakes,** a string of five lakes protected as a provincial recreation area. The lakes lie in a beautiful spot, with birdlife prolific and the waters stocked annually with rainbow trout. From the boat launch, a rough trail leads 1.6 kilometers (one mile) along the lakeshore to the site of a trading post. Camping is $20 per night.

Grande Cache and Vicinity

Grande Cache is a remote town of 3,700, 450 kilometers (280 miles) west of Edmonton and 182 kilometers (113 miles) south of Grande Prairie. The surrounding wilderness is totally undeveloped, offering endless opportunities for hiking, canoeing, kayaking, fishing, and horseback riding.

The first Europeans to explore the area were fur trappers and traders, who cached furs near

the site of the present town before taking them to major trading posts. At one point there was a small trading post on a lake south of town on Pierre Gray Lakes; its remains are still visible. Grande Cache is a planned town. Construction started in 1969 in response to a need for services and housing for miners and their families working at the Grande Cache Coal Corporation mine. The town was developed

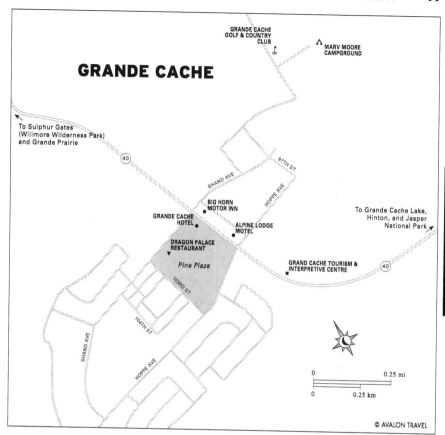

GRANDE CACHE

To Sulphur Gates
(Willmore Wilderness Park)
and Grande Prairie

40

GRANDE CACHE
GOLF & COUNTRY
CLUB

MARV MOORE
CAMPGROUND

97TH ST

SHAND AVE

HOPPE AVE

BIG HORN
MOTOR INN

GRANDE CACHE
HOTEL

ALPINE LODGE
MOTEL

DRAGON PALACE
RESTAURANT

Pine Plaza

To Grande Cache Lake,
Hinton, and Jasper
National Park

GRAND CACHE TOURISM &
INTERPRETIVE CENTRE

40

103RD ST

104TH ST

SHAND AVE

HOPPE AVE

0   0.25 mi

0   0.25 km

© AVALON TRAVEL

NORTHERN ALBERTA

20 kilometers (12.4 miles) south of the mine to maintain a scenic environment.

GRANDE CACHE TOURISM AND INTERPRETIVE CENTRE

This center (780/827-3300 or 888/827-3790, 9 A.M.–7 P.M. daily in summer, 9 A.M.–5 P.M. Mon.–Sat. the rest of the year) is outstanding, not just considering the size of the town that it represents, but for the wealth of information contained within it. It's easy to spend at least one hour in the two-story complex, with displays that include information about the human history of the region, the local industry, taxidermy, tree identification, and Willmore Wilderness Park. Other features

include an information desk, a gift shop, and a large deck from where views extend across the Smoky River Valley to the highest peaks of the Canadian Rockies. Beside it are a 1942 ranger cabin and a few picnic tables.

RECREATION

Most of the serious hiking and horseback riding takes place in adjacent Willmore Wilderness Park, but a variety of other recreational opportunities exist outside the park. For great views of the surrounding area, consider climbing **Grande Mountain.** It's a steep trail, gaining 730 meters (2,400 feet) of elevation in 3.5 kilometers (2.1 miles), but from the summit the view across the Smoky River

Valley to the Rocky Mountains is spectacular. The trail follows a power line the entire way to the peak and is easy to follow. To get to the trailhead, head northwest of town one kilometer (0.6 mile) and turn right at the cemetery gate. Park, walk along the road to the power line, veer right, and start the long slog to the summit. **Grande Cache Lake,** five kilometers (3.1 miles) south of town, has good swimming, canoeing, and fishing for rainbow trout. Longtime local Terry Deamer operates **Taste of Wilderness Tours** (780/827-4250, www.tasteofwilderness.ab.ca), with guided hiking ranging from nature walks (from $50) to heli-hiking (from $350). **Grande Cache Golf and Country Club** (780/827-5151, $32) is only nine holes, but you'll want to go around twice, however badly you're playing, because the scenery is distracting to say the least.

In recent years, Grande Cache has placed itself on the calendar of extreme ultra-marathoners the world over as host of the early-August **Canadian Death Race** (www.canadiandeathrace.com). The footrace takes place along a super-demanding 125-kilometer (78-mile) course, which summits three peaks.

ACCOMMODATIONS AND CAMPING

Because fewer than 250 rooms are available in the whole town, reservations should be made in advance. On the highway through town, the **Big Horn Motor Inn** (780/827-3744 or 888/880-2444, www.bighorninn.com, $90 s, $100 d) is the best value. Each of 37 rooms has a small fridge and wireless Internet, some have kitchenettes, and a laundry room and a restaurant are on the premises. Also along the highway is the similarly priced **Alpine Lodge Motel** (780/827-2450). If you're looking for something a little different, consider a stay at **Sheep Creek Back Country Lodge & Cabins** (780/831-1087 or 877/945-3786, www.sheepcreek.net, mid-June–mid-Sept., $95–110 s or d), which is accessed by a short walking trail and a suspension bridge from 24 kilometers (15 miles) north of town. It attracts an eclectic array of guests—anglers, hunters, mountain bikers—but everyone is welcome. Each rustic cabin has a simple kitchen, bedroom, deck, chemical toilet, and gravity-fed shower. A communal fridge/freezer is located in the main building. Guests bring their own food and towels.

Campgrounds

The only camping right in town is at **Marv Moore Campground** (780/827-2404, mid-May–mid-Oct., unserviced sites $20, powered sites $25), which has semiprivate, well-shaded sites and showers, kitchen shelters, a laundry, and firewood. It's at the north end of town on Shand Avenue beside the golf course. Four forestry campgrounds at regular intervals along Highway 40 are managed by North of 40 Wilderness Campgrounds (780/827-6521). Of special note is the one at the south end of **Sulphur Gates Provincial Recreation Area** (west off Hwy. 40 north of town, May–Oct., $20), which makes a good base for exploring adjacent Willmore Wilderness Park. It has just 10 sites.

FOOD

On a clear day, the view from the **Mountainview Family Restaurant** (Grande Cache Hotel, 1701 Pine Plaza, 780/827-3377, 5:30 A.M.–9 P.M. daily) is worth at least the price of a coffee. Soup-and-sandwich lunch specials are approximately $8, and pizza and pasta dishes start at $10. At the back of the hotel is **Rockies Bar and Grill,** with a regular bar menu and occasional live music. Across the plaza is **Dragon Palace Restaurant** (780/827-3898, 11 A.M.–10 P.M. daily). This is your quintessential small-town Chinese restaurant, with big portions of all the usual westernized Chinese favorites. All mains except the seafood dishes are under $10. Up on the highway, the **Big Horn Motor Inn** (780/827-3744) has a restaurant that opens at 5:30 A.M. daily.

INFORMATION AND SERVICES

The excellent **Grande Cache Tourism and Interpretive Centre** (780/827-3300 or

888/827-3790, www.visitgrandecache.com, 9 A.M.–7 P.M. daily in summer, 9 A.M.–5 P.M. Mon.–Sat. the rest of the year) is a great source of park information.

The **post office** is in the plaza, as is a laundry (beside IGA). **Home Hardware,** in the Pine Plaza, stocks camping and fishing gear.

WILLMORE WILDERNESS PARK

Willmore Wilderness Park is a northern extension of Jasper National Park. It lies south and west of Grande Cache, a small town on Highway 40 between Hinton and Grande Prairie. The 460,000-hectare (1,137,000-acre) wilderness is divided roughly in half by the Smoky River. The area west of the river is reached from Sulphur Gates. The east side is far less traveled—the terrain is rougher and wetter. The park is accessible only on foot, horseback, or, in winter, on skis. It is totally undeveloped—the trails that do exist are not maintained and in most cases are those once used by trappers.

The park is made up of long green ridges above the tree line and, farther west, wide passes and expansive basins along the Continental Divide. Lower elevations are covered in lodgepole pine and spruce, while at higher elevations the cover changes to fir. The diverse wildlife is one of the park's main attractions; white-tailed and mule deer, mountain goats, bighorn sheep, moose, elk, caribou, and black bears are all common. The park is also home to wolves, cougars, and grizzly bears.

Park Access and Travel

The easiest way to access the park is from Sulphur Gates Provincial Recreation Area, six kilometers (3.7 miles) north of Grande Cache on Highway 40 and then a similar distance along a gravel road to the west. Those not planning a trip into the park can still enjoy the cliffs at **Sulphur Gates** (formerly known as Hell's Gate), which is only a short walk from the end of the road. These 70-meter (230-foot) cliffs are at the confluence of the Sulphur and Smoky Rivers. The color difference between the glacial-fed Smoky River and spring-fed Sulphur River is apparent as they merge.

One of the most popular overnight trips from Sulphur Gates is to **Clarke's Cache,** an easy 16-kilometer (10-mile) hike to the remains of a cabin where trappers once stored furs before taking them to trading posts farther afield. A good option for a day trip for fit hikers is to the 2,013-meter (6,600-foot) summit of **Mount Stearn** from a trailhead 3.5 kilometers (2.2 miles) along the access road to Sulphur Gates. The trail begins by climbing alongside a stream through montane, then subalpine forest, and then through open meadows before reentering the forest and forking and rejoining. The official trail then climbs steeply and continuously to Lightning Ridge (10 km/6.2 miles one-way), but an easier summit is reached by heading up through the grassed slopes to a summit knob, 6.5 kilometers (four miles) and 1,000 vertical meters (3,280 vertical feet) from the road; allow 6–6.5 hours for the round-trip.

Practicalities

Anyone planning an extended trip into the park should be aware that no services are available, most trails are unmarked, and certain areas are heavily used by horse-packers. **High Country Vacations** (780/827-3246 or 877/487-2457, www.packtrails.com) offers pack trips into the park; expect to pay around $235 per person per day, all-inclusive. Get a taste of the park with **Taste of Wilderness Tours** (780/827-4250, www.tasteofwilderness.ab.ca), which offers day and overnight hikes within the park.

More information is available by visiting www.wilmorewildernesspark.com, which represents local outfitters.

TO GRANDE PRAIRIE

From Grande Cache, a 181-kilometer (112-mile) gravel road follows the Smoky River out of the foothills and into the wide valley in which Grande Prairie lies. Along the route are service campgrounds and good opportunities for wildlife viewing.

NORTHERN ALBERTA

Grande Prairie and Vicinity

Grande Prairie, a city of 51,000, is in a wide, gently rolling valley surrounded by large areas of natural grasslands. Edmonton is 460 kilometers (286 miles) to the southeast, while Dawson Creek (British Columbia) and Mile Zero of the Alaska Highway are 135 kilometers (84 miles) to the northwest. Grasslands are something of an anomaly at such a northern latitude. To the south and west are heavily forested mountains, and to the north and east are boreal forests and wetlands. But the grasslands here, *la grande prairie,* provided the stimulus for growth in the region. Although so many of Alberta's northern towns began and grew as trading posts beside rivers, Grande Prairie grew as a result of the land's agricultural potential.

In the late 1800s, when the first settlers began making the arduous journey north to Peace River Country, the area had no roads and no communication to the outside world. Families had to be entirely self-sufficient. But that didn't deter the first immigrants from journeying through 300 kilometers (186 miles) of dense forests and boggy muskeg to the prairie, which was isolated from southern farmland but highly suited to agriculture. When the Grand Trunk Pacific Railway reached Edson, to the south, settlers arrived over the **Edson Trail.** When the railway arrived from Dunvegan in 1916, the settlement—then on the floodplains of Bear Creek—boomed. The population continued to climb slowly but steadily until 1976, when the discovery of Alberta's largest gas reserve nearby boosted it to more than 20,000. Now the largest city in northwestern Alberta, Grande Prairie is a service, cultural, and transportation center.

SIGHTS

Although malls, motels, restaurants, and other services are spread out along Highway 2 west and north of town, the center of the city has managed to retain much of its original charm. A short walk west of downtown on 100th Avenue is **Bear Creek,** along which most of Grande Prairie's sights lie.

Muskoseepi Park

Muskoseepi (Bear Creek, in the Cree language) is a 405-hectare (1,000-acre) park that preserves a wide swathe of land through the heart of the city. At the north end of the park is **Bear Creek Reservoir,** the focal point of the park. Here you'll find an interpretive pavilion, a heated outdoor pool, tennis courts, minigolf, and canoe rentals ($12 per hour). At the magnificent open-plan **Centre 2000,** Grande Prairie's main information center, a stairway leads up to the **Northern Lights Lookout.** From Centre 2000, 40 kilometers (25 miles) of hiking and biking trails follow both sides of Bear Creek to the city's outer edge.

Overlooking the reservoir (access from the Highway 2 bypass) is **Grande Prairie Regional College.** Designed by renowned architect Douglas Cardinal, the flowing curves of this brick building are the city's most distinctive landmark.

Grande Prairie Museum

Located in Muskoseepi Park and overlooking Bear Creek, this excellent museum (780/532-5482, 8:30 A.M.–4:30 P.M. Mon.–Fri., 10 A.M.–4:30 P.M. Sat., noon–4:30 P.M. Sun., adult $5, senior $4, child $3) is within easy walking distance (30 minutes) of Centre 2000 along Bear Creek. If you're driving, access is east along 102nd Avenue from downtown. Indoor displays include the Heritage Discovery Centre, which catalogs the area's early development through interactive exhibits, a natural history display, and dinosaur bones from a nearby dig site. Historic buildings outside include a church, a schoolhouse, a blacksmith shop, and a fire station.

Prairie Art Gallery

Housed in the Montrose Cultural Centre, this large gallery (9839 103rd Ave., 780/532-8111,

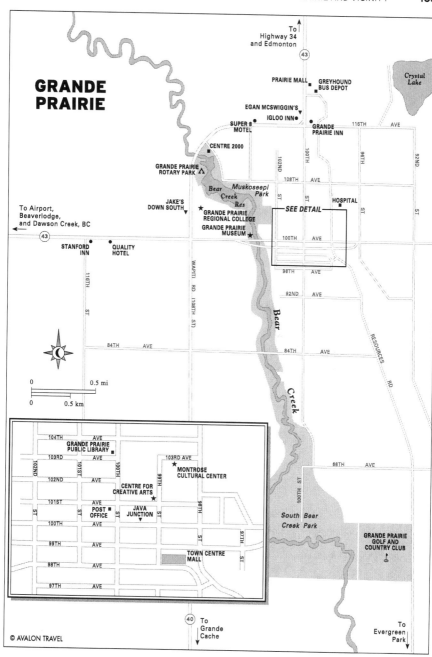

GRANDE PRAIRIE

To Highway 34 and Edmonton

Crystal Lake

PRAIRIE MALL   GREYHOUND BUS DEPOT

EGAN MCSWIGGIN'S
IGLOO INN

SUPER 8 MOTEL   GRANDE PRAIRIE INN

CENTRE 2000

GRANDE PRAIRIE ROTARY PARK

Muskoseepi Park
Bear Creek
Res

JAKE'S DOWN SOUTH
GRANDE PRAIRIE REGIONAL COLLEGE
GRANDE PRAIRIE MUSEUM

To Airport, Beaverlodge, and Dawson Creek, BC

STANFORD INN   QUALITY HOTEL

SEE DETAIL

HOSPITAL

Bear Creek

116TH   AVE
108TH   AVE
100TH   AVE
98TH   AVE
92ND   AVE
84TH   AVE

102ND ST   100TH ST   96TH ST   92ND ST
116TH ST
WAPITI RD (108TH ST)

RESOURCES RD

84TH   AVE

68TH   AVE

South Bear Creek Park

GRANDE PRAIRIE GOLF AND COUNTRY CLUB

0   0.5 mi
0   0.5 km

NORTHERN ALBERTA

Detail inset:

104TH   AVE
GRANDE PRAIRIE PUBLIC LIBRARY
103RD   AVE   103RD AVE
MONTROSE CULTURAL CENTER
102ND   AVE
CENTRE FOR CREATIVE ARTS
101ST   AVE
POST OFFICE   JAVA JUNCTION
100TH   AVE
99TH   AVE
98TH   AVE
TOWN CENTRE MALL
97TH   AVE

102ND ST   101ST   100TH   99TH ST   98TH ST   97TH ST

40 To Grande Cache

To Evergreen Park

© AVALON TRAVEL

10 A.M.–8 P.M. Mon.–Thurs., 10 A.M.–6 P.M. Fri.–Sat., 2–5 P.M. Sun., free), fills an imposing 1920s high school building, with galleries spilling into a modern addition. Over 500 works of art by artists from across Canada are displayed in permanent and temporary exhibitions.

Kleskun Hill Natural Area

Kleskun Hill, 20 kilometers (12.5 miles) east of Grande Prairie along Highway 34, is the most northern badlands in North America. Approximately 70 million years ago, the land around these parts was a river delta, which today rises 100 meters (330 feet) above the surrounding prairie. Plant species normally associated with southern latitudes, such as prickly pear cactus, are found here. The only facility is a picnic area at the south end.

RECREATION
Golf

Grande Prairie has several challenging and well-maintained golf courses. Greens fees range $32–55. My favorite is 6,450-yard-long **The Dunes** (780/538-4333 or 888/224-2252), on the Wapiti River, seven kilometers (4.3 miles) south of the city. It features two distinct "nines," the first with tree-lined fairways, the second wide open in the style of a Scottish links course. Also south of the city are **Grande Prairie Golf and Country Club** (780/532-0333) and **Bear Creek Golf Club** (780/538-3393), which has an RV park.

ENTERTAINMENT AND EVENTS
Theater

Two theaters offer performances September–April. **Grande Prairie Live Theatre,** based at the renovated Second Street Theatre (10130 98th Ave., 780/538-1616), is small, but all productions are popular. **Douglas J. Cardinal Performing Arts Centre** (10726 106th Ave., 780/539-2911) hosts amateur dramas as well as touring performers and country-music stars.

Festivals and Events

Evergreen Park, south of downtown, hosts many of the city's larger events, including a farmers market each Saturday during summer, horse racing, demolition derbies, and fall harvest festivals. The weekend closest to May 31 is **Grande Prairie Stompede** (780/532-4646, www.gpstompede.com), a gathering of North America's best cowboys and chuck wagon drivers. The regional fair, with a livestock show, chuck wagon races, and a midway, is the last weekend of July. For further information on these events, call the park administration (780/532-3279). Muskoseepi Park hosts **National Aboriginal Day** on the fourth weekend of June.

ACCOMMODATIONS AND CAMPING

All motels are located west and north of downtown along Highway 2; the first two listed are to the west, whereas the others line the northern approach to the city.

Grande Prairie Stanford Hotel (11401 100th Ave., 780/539-5678 or 800/661-8160, www.grandeprairiestanfordhotel.com, $130 s, $135 d) is a large 204-room complex with midsize guest rooms, a fitness room, an outdoor hot tub, Delmonica's Restaurant, and a bar. The **Quality Hotel** (11201 100th Ave., 780/539-6000 or 800/661-7954, www.choicehotels.ca, $135 s or d) stands out not only for its sleek exterior, but also inside for modern, well-designed rooms with all the amenities. A fitness center, business center, restaurant, and lounge are on-site. Rates include local calls, a light breakfast, and an airport shuttle. **Grande Prairie Inn** (11633 100th St., 780/532-5221 or 800/661-6529, www.gpinn.com, $139–169 s or d) is a full-service hotel right at the Highway 2 bypass. Facilities include an indoor pool, a restaurant, a lounge, and a nightclub. Don't expect any surprises at the **Super 8 Motel** (10050 116th Ave., 780/532-8288 or 800/800-8000, www.super8.com, $139 s or d)—just the usual high standard of reliable rooms, an indoor pool and waterslide, a laundry facility, and a free continental breakfast.

Campgrounds

Grande Prairie Rotary Park (along the Hwy.

2 bypass, 780/532-1137, May–Sept.) overlooks Bear Creek and is just across from Centre 2000. It has showers and a laundry room but few trees; tent sites down by the water are $20, RVs and trailers pay $28–35 (no reservations taken).

FOOD

The dining scene in Grande Prairie is unremarkable at best. **Jake's Down South** (10702 108th St., 780/532-5667, 11 A.M.–10 P.M. daily, $15–27) doesn't look like much from the outside, but the Southern-style food is as good as you're likely to come across in Grande Prairie. Think jambalaya ($19) and blackened catfish ($19). Across the road, the Grande Prairie Regional College has a cafeteria that bustles with students (and locals looking for a cheap meal) throughout the school year.

Egan McSwiggin's (upstairs at 11920 100th St., 780/402-7090) has a refined Irish-pub atmosphere with a cross-section of British fare on a long menu. The Grande Prairie Inn (11633 Clairmont Rd., 780/532-5221) holds the **Drake's Nest Café** (6:30 A.M.–2 P.M. and 4–10 P.M. daily), offering weekday lunch buffets for $16.95 per person. **Delmonica's** (Grande Prairie Stanford Hotel, 11401 100th Ave., 780/539-5678, breakfast, lunch, and dinner daily) is another hotel dining room with a lunchtime buffet.

INFORMATION AND SERVICES

Overlooking Bear Creek Reservoir, **Centre 2000** (off the Hwy. 2 bypass at 11330 106th St., 780/539-7688, 8:30 A.M.–7 P.M. daily May–Sept., 8:30 A.M.–4:30 P.M. daily the rest of the year) houses the local tourist information center. One desk is staffed by Travel Alberta employees while an adjacent space is dedicated to supplying local information. Another source of information is the Grande Prairie Tourism website (www.gptourism.ca).

Part of the Montrose Cultural Centre, **Grande Prairie Public Library** (9839 103rd Ave., 780/532-3580) is a modern facility with wireless Internet access and regular modem-connected computers. It's open 10 A.M.–9 P.M.

Monday–Thursday, 10 A.M.–6 P.M. Friday–Saturday, and 2–5 P.M. Sunday.

The **post office** is at 10001 101st Avenue. **Towne Centre Laundry** is in the Towne Centre Mall at 99th Avenue and 100th Street. **Queen Elizabeth II Hospital** (780/538-7100) is at 10409 98th Street.

GETTING THERE AND AROUND

Grande Prairie Airport (2 km/1.2 miles west of downtown, then north along Airport Rd.) is served by **Air Canada** and **WestJet;** both have daily flights to Calgary and Edmonton.

The **Greyhound** bus depot (9918 121st Ave., 780/539-1111 or 800/661-8747, www.greyhound.ca) has a café and lockers. Buses leave four times daily to Edmonton, once daily to Peace River, and twice daily to Dawson Creek (British Columbia).

For a taxi, call **Prairie Cabs** (780/532-1060) or **Swan Taxi** (780/539-4000).

VICINITY OF GRANDE PRAIRIE
Saskatoon Island Provincial Park

For thousands of years, natives have come to this area to collect, as the name suggests, Saskatoon berries. The "Island" part of the name dates to the 1920s, when much of what is now protected was an island; today the park is an isthmus between Little and Saskatoon Lakes. Sweet, purple-colored Saskatoon berries are still abundant and cover nearly one-third of the 102-hectare (250-acre) park. Late July and August are the best times for berry picking, although park rangers don't encourage the activity. **Little Lake,** with its abundant aquatic vegetation, provides an ideal habitat for trumpeter swans, North America's largest waterfowl. This park is one of the few areas in Canada where the majestic bird can be viewed during the spring nesting season. Vegetation in the park is classified as northern aspen parkland, the only park in Alberta to represent this biome.

The campground (780/538-5350, May–Sept., unserviced sites $20, powered sites $26)

NORTHERN ALBERTA

has showers, groceries, a food concession, and minigolf, and is beside a beach. Around half of the 103 sites have power, so arrive early in the day (especially on Friday) if you require hook-ups. The park is 20 kilometers (12.5 miles) west of Grande Prairie on Highway 2, then three kilometers (1.9 miles) north.

Beaverlodge and Vicinity

This small town, 40 kilometers (25 miles) west of Grande Prairie along Highway 2, is a northern agricultural center at the gateway to **Monkman Pass,** a pass through the Canadian Rockies found earlier in the 20th century. The only access to the pass is by four-wheel-drive vehicle. Two kilometers (1.2 miles) northwest from Beaverlodge, the **South Peace Centennial Museum** (780/354-8869, 10 A.M.–6 P.M. daily mid-May–early Sept., adult $5) started as a farmer's hobby and has grown into a working museum cataloging the agricultural history of Alberta, with displays housed in 15 buildings. Highlights include restored steam-powered farm equipment and a steam-driven sawmill. On

Pioneer Day, the third Sunday of July, all of the farm machinery is started up and operated.

Sexsmith

North of Grande Prairie, the small town of Sexsmith—once known as the Grain Capital of the British Empire—has undergone extensive restoration. Its main street is now a pleasant place to stop, with most businesses fronted by early-1900s-style facades. One block off the main street is the **Sexsmith Blacksmith Shop** (780/568-3668, 9:30 A.M.–4:30 P.M. Mon.–Fri., 10 A.M.–4 P.M. Sat.–Sun. June–early Sept.), a working museum restored to its original 1916 condition. Inside the log structure are more than 10,000 artifacts, including caches of moonshine, which were hidden in the log walls to prevent detection by the NWMP.

From Sexsmith, Highway 2 climbs slowly through a mixed-wood forest connecting the Saddle Hills, to the west, and the Birch Hills, to the northeast. After crossing a low, indistinguishable summit, the road begins descending into the Peace River Valley.

Peace River Valley

From its source in the interior of British Columbia, the Peace River has carved a majestic swath across the northwestern corner of Alberta's boreal forest. Explorers, trappers, settlers, and missionaries traveled upstream from Fort Chipewyan on Lake Athabasca and established trading posts along the fertile valley and surrounding plains. The posts at Fort Vermilion and Dunvegan have slipped into oblivion and are now designated as historic sites, but the town of Peace River has grown from a small post into an agriculture and distribution center that serves the entire Peace River region. The river—so named because on its banks peace was made between warring Cree and Beaver Indians—and the surrounding land are often referred to as Peace Country. This moniker is a throwback to the 1930s, when the government refused to build a rail link and many

local residents favored seceding from Alberta and creating their own country.

UPPER PEACE VALLEY

The Upper Peace Valley extends 230 kilometers (143 miles) from the Alberta–British Columbia border to the town of Peace River. From Highway 49, on the south side of the river, and Highways 64 and 2 on the north side, roads lead down to the river and nine recreation and camping areas, initially developed for the bicentennial of Alexander Mackenzie's historic passage to the Pacific Ocean.

Moonshine Lake Provincial Park and Vicinity

More than 100 species of birds and, in winter, high concentrations of moose call Moonshine Lake Provincial Park home. Occupying 1,080 hectares (2,670 acres) 42 kilometers (26 miles) west of Rycroft, the park is best known for its rainbow trout fishing. Some people claim that the lake is named for the moon's reflection on its still water, although it more likely came from a fellow who sold moonshine to travelers en route to Dawson Creek. The campground (780/538-5350, mid-May–mid-Sept., unserviced sites $20, powered sites $26, no reservations taken) has over 100 sites scattered among stands of aspen, poplar, and white spruce. Amenities include showers, flush toilets, kitchen shelters, a concession, and firewood.

From south of the park, Highway 49 continues 54 kilometers (34 miles) to the Alberta–British Columbia border and another 19 kilometers (12 miles) to Dawson Creek at Mile Zero of the Alaska Highway.

◖ Historic Dunvegan

As Highway 2 descends into the Peace River Valley from the south, it crosses Alberta's longest suspension bridge at Dunvegan—a point that was the site of many trading posts and a mission. On the north side of the river is the **Visitor Reception Centre** (780/835-7150, 10 A.M.–6 P.M. daily mid-May–early Sept., adult $3, senior $2, child $1.50), featuring displays that tell the story of Dunvegan and its role in the early history of northern Alberta. On the riverbank are the restored church and rectory of the St. Charles Roman Catholic Mission, circa 1885 (look for the gnarled maple tree, planted by early missionaries, behind the mission site). A gravel road leads under the bridge to the site of the original settlement, **Fort Dunvegan,** which was built as a trading post for the North West Company in 1805, and in use until 1918. Nothing but depressions in the ground remain from the original settlement, but set back from the road is a white Hudson's Bay Company factor's house. Adjacent to these historic sites is **Dunvegan Provincial Park** (780/538-5350, mid-May–mid-Oct., powered sites $26), where all 67 sites are powered.

Highway 64

From **Fairview,** 26 kilometers (16 miles) northeast of Dunvegan, Highway 64 heads north then west, roughly following the Peace River into British Columbia. Along the way is the town of **Hines Creek** and its **End of Steel Museum** (780/494-3991, 10 A.M.–5 P.M. daily June–Aug., donation) featuring a caboose, a church, a trapper's cabin, and a Russian pioneer home. From Hines Creek, it is 98 kilometers (61 miles) to the British Columbia border.

PEACE RIVER

From all directions, the final approach into the town of Peace River is breathtaking. This town of 6,200 straddles the majestic Peace River below the confluence of the Smoky and Heart Rivers. Alexander Mackenzie was one of the earliest white men to visit the region. He established a post, named Fort Forks, on the south bank of the river, upstream of the present town. From here, after the winter of 1792–1793, he completed his historic journey to the Pacific Ocean and became the first person to cross the North American continent north of Mexico. The first permanent settlers were missionaries who, apart from their zealous religious work, promoted the region for its agricultural potential and as a service center and distribution point for river transportation. When the rail link with Edmonton was completed in 1916, land was opened for homesteading, and settlers poured into town. The farming traditions they began continue on.

Sights

Many historic buildings line the main street (100th Street), and many have plaques with historical facts. The wide street is typical of early boomtowns in that its width allowed wagons to turn around. At the southern end of the street, across the mouth of the Heart River, is the **Peace River Museum** (10302 99th St., 780/624-4261, 10:30 A.M.–4 P.M. Mon.–Sat., adult $3), which has three galleries filled with displays on native clothing, the fur trade, Alexander Mackenzie and other early explorers, and the development of the town.

Two spots near downtown afford excellent views of the Peace River and the valley through which it flows. To access the closest,

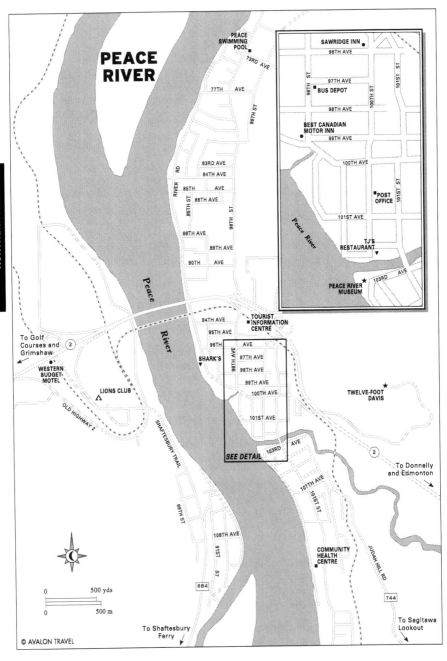

© AVALON TRAVEL

TWELVE-FOOT DAVIS

Pathfinder, pioneer, miner, trader. He was every man's friend and never locked his cabin door.

This fitting tribute adorns the headstone of Twelve-Foot Davis, one of the early pioneers of the Peace River Country.

Born Henry Fuller Davis in Vermont in 1820, Twelve-Foot was not a giant of a man. In fact, he was short. But he got his name from a claim he staked in the Cariboo goldfields in British Columbia. He noticed that two very successful claims had a 12-foot strip between them, so he staked the area and made a fortune. Although he was illiterate, Davis saw potential in selling supplies to the miners. He arrived in the Peace River Country in the 1870s, opening up trading posts as far apart as Hudson's Hope (British Columbia) and Fort Vermilion, but spending most of his later years running a post at Dunvegan. Davis was renowned for his hospitality, handing out sage advice to newcomers and baking pumpkin pies (a real treat in the north) for homesick Americans. He died at Grouard in 1900, and in accordance with his dying wishes, he now lies buried high above his beloved river (access from 100th Avenue, and under Highway 2).

© ANDREW HEMPSTEAD

NORTHERN ALBERTA

take 100th Avenue under Highway 2 and follow this winding road to its end, or, alternatively, take 101st Street south to 107th Avenue, which links up with Judah Hill Road. This road passes **Sagitawa Lookout,** from where you can see the town, the valley, and the confluence of the Peace and Smoky Rivers.

On the west side of the river is the site of **Shaftesbury,** a settlement that grew around an Anglican mission founded in 1887. From the site, Highway 684 follows the historic Shaftesbury Trail—used for hundreds of years by natives, explorers, traders, missionaries, and Klondikers—to Blakely's Landing, from which the free **Shaftesbury Ferry** now crosses the river all summer, 7 A.M.–midnight daily, carrying a maximum of eight vehicles.

Tours

Peace Island Tours (780/624-4295, www.peaceisland.ab.ca) operates jet-boat trips, departing at 2 P.M., that head 60 kilometers (37 miles) down the Peace River to a 14-hectare (35-acre) island with log cabins. The seven-hour Supper Tour is $90 per person, whereas the overnight journey, including three meals, the boat ride, and lodging, is $170 per person.

Accommodations and Camping

The least-expensive rooms in town are at the **Western Budget Motel** (7701 100th Ave., 780/624-3445, www.westernbudgetmotel.com, $89 s, $99 d). It may be across the river from downtown, but the rooms are comfortable, and there's an on-site restaurant. At the **Best**

NORTHERN ALBERTA

Canadian Motor Inn (9810 98th St., 780/624-2586 or 888/700-2264, www.bestcdn.com, $93 s, $103 d), upgrade to a kitchenette for $113 or the larger suites for $125. At the north end of downtown but still within walking distance of everything is the 142-room **Sawridge Inn** (9510 100th St., 780/624-3621 or 888/729-7343, www.sawridgepeaceriver.com, $126–140 s or d), where the rooms come in a variety of configurations. This hotel has a fitness room, restaurant (open from 5:30 A.M. daily), and a lounge.

Lions Club Park (on the west side of the river, 780/624-2120, Apr.–Oct., unserviced sites $20, hookups $25–30) has well-shaded campsites, showers, and a laundry room.

Food

Restaurant choices are limited. Try busy **TJ's Restaurant** (10011 102nd Ave., 780/624-3427, breakfast, lunch, and dinner daily, $8–13), where the Chinese dishes are better than the Canadian and there's generally a daily pasta special. Especially delicious is the Seafood Hotpot ($16). **Alexander's** (9510 100th St., 780/624-3621, 5:30 A.M.–10 P.M. daily, $12–18), in the Sawridge Inn, offers reasonably creative fare, such as prawn and strawberry salad and hearty favorites like lasagna. Pizzas are also recommended. Both the breakfast buffet ($11) and lunch buffet ($14) are a good value. In the same hotel is **Shark's,** a sports lounge with a wide-ranging menu to match.

Information

The **Mighty Peace Tourist Association** operates a tourist information center (780/338-2364 or 800/215-4535, www.mightypeace.com, 10 A.M.–6 P.M. daily June–Sept.) in the old Peace River railway station at the top end of 100th Street.

MACKENZIE HIGHWAY

Named for 18th-century explorer Alexander Mackenzie, this route, also known as Highway 35, extends from Grimshaw, 24 kilometers (15 miles) west of Peace River, for 473 kilometers (294 miles) north to the Northwest Territories. It passes through a vast, empty land dominated by the Peace River and a seemingly endless forest of spruce, poplar, and jack pine. The main

AURORA BOREALIS

The aurora borealis, or northern lights, is an emotional experience for some, spiritual for others, and without exception is unforgettable – an exhibition of color that dances across the sky like a kaleidoscope.

Auroral light is created through a complex process – a spontaneous phenomenon with no pattern and no "season" – that occurs within Earth's atmosphere and starts with the sun. Essentially a huge atomic fusion reactor, the sun emits the heat and light that keep us alive and also emits electronically charged ions that are thrust through space at high speeds. When these ions reach Earth's rarefied upper atmosphere – about 180 kilometers (112 miles) above the surface – they are captured by Earth's magnetic field and accelerated toward the poles. Along the way they collide with the

atoms and molecules of the gases in the atmosphere, which in turn become temporarily charged or "ionized." This absorbed energy is then released by the ionized gases, often in the form of light. The color of the light varies from red to yellow to green, depending on the gas: Nitrogen atoms produce a violet and sometimes a red color, oxygen a green and, at higher altitudes, an orange.

Because the magnetic field is more intense near the north and south magnetic poles, the lights are best seen at high latitudes. In northern Alberta the light show takes place up to 160 nights annually, with displays best north of Peace River. They generally start as a faint glow on the northeastern horizon after the sun has set, improving as the sky becomes darker.

population centers are Manning and High Level. Along the way are many stump-filled fields, carved out of the boreal forest by farmers who, for the last 100 years, have eked out a living from some of the world's northernmost farmland. The only access to the Peace River is at Notikewin Provincial Park and at **Tompkin's Landing,** a ferry crossing east of Paddle Prairie.

When you're through exploring this wild northland, you have two alternatives to backtracking along Mackenzie Highway. One is to continue into the Northwest Territories and complete what is known as the **Deh Cho Connection,** which links the Mackenzie with the Liard and Alaska Highways—an 1,800-kilometer (1,200-mile) loop that finishes in Dawson Creek, British Columbia. The other option is to follow Highway 58 east from High Level and head south on the Bicentennial Highway 430 kilometers (267 miles) to Slave Lake.

Grimshaw

Best known as Mile Zero of the Mackenzie Highway, this town of 2,400 has grown around the railway as a farming center. For many years after the railway arrived, it was a jumping-off point for farmers, trappers, and homesteaders in Peace Valley Country. Make a point of stopping at the local information center (9 A.M.–5 P.M. daily June–early Sept.), in a blue rail car at the main intersection. It's stocked with brochures for onward travel and staffed by friendly locals who seem genuinely interested in your travels.

Camp at nearby Queen Elizabeth Provincial Park (780/624-6486, mid-May–mid-Oct., unserviced sites $20, powered sites $26) or continue 11 kilometers (6.8 miles) north to **The Creek Golf Course** (780/332-4949, May–Sept.), where camping with hookups and showers is $24 and a round of golf is $22.

Lac Cardinal

North of Grimshaw, on the eastern shore of Lac Cardinal, is **Queen Elizabeth Provincial Park.** The lake is very shallow, and no streams flow from it. This creates an ideal habitat for many species of waterfowl. Beavers, moose, and black bears are also present. The park campground (780/624-6486, mid-May–mid-Oct., unserviced sites $20, powered sites $26) has pit toilets, firewood, and kitchen shelters. Immediately south of the park is **Lac Cardinal Pioneer Village Museum** (780/332-2030, 11 A.M.–5 P.M. daily May–Sept., donation), featuring a large outdoor collection of memorabilia from the Peace River region.

To Manning

From Grimshaw, it is 40 kilometers (25 miles) north to the small hamlet of **Dixonville.** Here you'll find a trading post and the turnoff to Sulphur Lake (55 km/34 miles northwest along Hwy. 689), where camping is available.

A homestead built by a Latvian settler in 1918 is three kilometers (1.9 miles) south of **North Star,** on the old Highway 35. It has been declared a Provincial Historic Site, and although it's locked, you can look in the windows and see homemade wooden beds and a sauna, and appreciate the work that went into the hand-hewn log buildings.

Manning

As the highway descends into the picturesque Notikewin Valley, it passes through the relatively new town of Manning. Formerly called Aurora, this town of 1,200 is a service center for the region's agricultural and petroleum industries. At the south end of town, one kilometer (0.6 mile) east on Highway 691, is the excellent **Battle River Pioneer Museum** (780/836-2374, 1–6 P.M. daily May–Sept., from 10 A.M. in July and Aug., adult $3, child $1), which has a large collection of antique wrenches, taxidermy (including a rare albino moose), carriages and buggies, farm machinery, a birch necklace carved out of a single piece of wood, and a collection of prehistoric arrowheads—ask to see the one embedded in a whalebone.

Manning Motor Inn (780/836-2801, $109 s, $119 d) is at the south end of town and has a restaurant. **Manning Riverside Campground** (May–Sept., $20) is immediately west of the tourist information center in a shaded spot beside the Notikewin River. The campground is small (nine sites) but has some powered sites. It is also possible to camp at the golf course, north of town (780/836-2176, May–Sept., $20), which offers powered sites and a clubhouse restaurant. The **Old Hospital Gallery & Museum** (780/836-3606, 10 A.M.–5 P.M. Mon.–Sat. May–Sept., free) combines historical displays related to the building with an art gallery and the local information center.

Notikewin Provincial Park

Twenty-one kilometers (13 miles) north of Hotchkiss, Highway 692 turns east off Highway 35 and leads to Notikewin Provincial Park, a 970-hectare (2,400-acre) preserve at the confluence of the Notikewin and Peace Rivers. The 30-kilometer (19-mile) road to the park is partly paved and occasionally steep. In Notikewin (Battle, in the Cree language), a stand of 200-year-old spruce presides over Spruce Island, at the mouth of the Notikewin River. The island also supports an abundance of ostrich ferns growing to a height of two meters (six feet). Beaver, mule deer, moose, and the occasional black bear can be seen in the area. Bird species are diverse and include sandhill cranes, which rest at the mouth of the Notikewin River on their southern migration in September. The river offers good fishing for goldeye, walleye, and northern pike. The campground (May–Oct., $20) has 19 sites but no hookups.

If you're looking for a spot to camp without detouring from Highway 35, continue 23 kilometers (14 miles) north to **Twin Lakes,** where camping is $17. Take time to walk the three-kilometer/1.9-mile (50-minute) circuit around the larger of the two lakes—it's a typical environment of boreal forest, and it has been unaffected by fire or deforestation for more than 80 years.

A Short Detour

The largest of eight Métis settlements established throughout the province during the 1930s is **Paddle Prairie,** 65 kilometers (40 miles) north of Twin Lakes. From 10 kilometers (6.2 miles) north of here, a gravel road (Highway 697) leads east to the Peace River and Tomkin's Landing and one of only eight ferry crossings in the province (operates daily 24 hours in summer). It then continues to La Crete and Fort Vermilion, crosses the Peace River, and intersects Highway 58, which heads west, rejoining the Mackenzie Highway at High Level.

La Crete (pop. 2,300) has grown into an agricultural center on the northern fringe of the continent's arable land. Most residents are Mennonites who moved to the region in the 1930s. They are from a traditional Protestant sect originating in Holland, whose members settled in remote regions throughout the world and established self-sufficient agricultural lifestyles, in hopes of being left to practice their faith in peace. On the streets and in the local restaurants, you'll hear their language, *Plattdeutsch* (Low German), which is spoken by Mennonites throughout the world.

To the southeast of this flat, prairielike area, the Buffalo Head Hills rise almost 700 meters (2,300 feet) above the surrounding land. The only way into the hills is along an 18-kilometer (11-mile) gravel road that spurs east from Highway 697 approximately 18 kilometers (11 miles) south of La Crete. To the west, an eight-kilometer (five-mile) road from town leads past a golf course to one of the Peace River's many natural sandbars, and to Etna's Landing, where there is good swimming.

Fort Vermilion

This town of 780, on the south bank of the Peace River, 40 kilometers (25 miles) north of La Crete and 77 kilometers (48 miles) east of High Level, vies with Fort Chipewyan as the oldest settlement in Alberta. It was named for the red clay deposits present in the banks of the river. The first trading post here was established a few kilometers downstream of present-day Fort Vermilion by the North West Company in 1788. Trade with the Beaver, Cree, and Dene was brisk, and by 1802 the Hudson's Bay Company had also established a post. In 1821, the companies merged, and in

1830 they moved operations to the town's present site. The area's agricultural potential gained worldwide attention when locally grown wheat, transported along the river highway, won a gold medal at the 1876 World's Fair in Philadelphia. For 150 years, supplies arrived by riverboat or were hauled overland from the town of Peace River. When the Mackenzie Highway was completed, the river highway became obsolete. The last riverboat arrived in Fort Vermilion in 1952, but not until 1974, when a bridge was built across the Peace River, was the town linked to the outside world.

Many old buildings and cabins, in varying states of disrepair, still stand. Pick up a *Fort Vermilion Heritage Guide* from the **Fort Vermilion Heritage Centre** (780/927-4603, 9 A.M.–9 P.M. Mon.–Thurs., 9 A.M.–5 P.M. Fri.–Sat., 1–9 P.M. Sun. June–Aug., donation) to help identify the many historic sites in town. The **Mary Batt & Son General Store** was constructed from logs removed from the 1897 Hudson's Bay Company post.

Across from the river, the **Sheridan Lawrence Inn** (4901 River Rd., 780/927-4400, $82 s, $89 d) is the only place to stay in town. It offers 16 rooms and a small restaurant open from 7 A.M. daily, with a predictable Canadian and Chinese menu.

High Level

Named for its location on a divide between the Peace and Hay River watersheds, High Level (pop. 4,100), 279 kilometers (173 miles) north of Grimshaw, is the last town before the Alberta–Northwest Territories border. It is a major service center for a region rich in natural resources. The town expanded during the oil boom of the 1960s and has prospered ever since. The grain elevators, serving agricultural communities to the east, are the northernmost in the world. Forestry is also a major local industry; the town boasts one of the world's most productive logging and sawmill operations, turning out more than 250 million board-feet of lumber annually.

Fortunately, much of the surrounding forest is safe from loggers; the 75,000-square-

kilometer (30,000-square-mile) **Footner Lake Forest** has poor drainage, forming major bogs and permafrost that make timber harvest commercially unviable. The forest encompasses the entire northern part of the province west of Wood Buffalo National Park.

Northeast of High Level are the **Caribou Mountains,** which rise to a forested plateau 800 meters (2,600 feet) above the Peace River. At that altitude, and being so far north, the fragile environment is easily disturbed. The mountains are blanketed in white spruce, aspen, and pine, and two lakes—Margaret and Wentzel—offer excellent fly-fishing. Northwest of High Level are the Cameron Hills and **Bistcho Lake** (where Albertan fish hatcheries harvest walleye spawn). The most accessible part of the forest is **Hutch Lake,** 32 kilometers (20 miles) north of town. The lake is surrounded by aspen and poplar and is the source of the **Meander River.** The dominant feature here is **Watt Mountain** (780 meters/2,600 feet), which you can see to the northwest of High Level. From Hutch Lake, a service road leads 10 kilometers (6.2 miles) to a lookout and 21 kilometers (13 miles) to a fire tower on the summit. The recreation area at the north end of the lake has a large picnic area, an interpretive trail, and camping. Maps are available at the tourist information center.

The only worthwhile sight in town is **Mackenzie Crossroads Museum** (at the south entrance to town, 780/926-2470, 9 A.M.–7 P.M. Mon.–Sat. May–Sept., 9 A.M.–5 P.M. Mon.–Fri. the rest of the year, adult $2, student $1). Located in the tourist information center building, the museum is themed on a northern trading post, with interesting displays telling the human history of northern Alberta. In another room, the industries upon which High Level was built are described through photographs and interpretive boards. A three-dimensional map of northwestern Alberta gives a great perspective of this inaccessible part of the province.

Motel prices in High Level are just a warm-up for those over the border in the Northwest Territories, so don't be surprised at

$80 rooms that you'd prefer to pay $40 for. The motels in town are usually full throughout the year with work crews. One of the least expensive is **Our Place Motel** (10402 97th St., 780/926-2556 or 866/926-3631, $79 s, $89 d), with an adjacent restaurant and wireless Internet throughout. **Best Canadian Motor Inn** (780/926-2272, www.bestcdn.com, $77 s, $87 d) undergoes regular revamps, and its medium-size rooms are air-conditioned. A free municipal campground is immediately east of town on Highway 35 (but it's pretty grotty), and a primitive campground lies farther north at **Hutch Lake Recreation Area** (mid-May–Sept., $13).

The **Family Restaurant** (in front of the Family Motel, 780/926-3111, breakfast, lunch, and dinner daily) offers a Chinese buffet lunch ($12) and a regular dinner menu with main meals from $10. Another Chinese place is the **Canton Restaurant** (100th Ave., 780/926-3053, lunch and dinner daily, $9–14); the combo dinners seem like a good deal, but portions are small, so stick to the main meals.

The post office, banks, library, and several launderettes are located on 100th Street.

Rainbow Lake

Rainbow Lake is an oil field community of 1,100, 141 kilometers (88 miles) west of High Level along Highway 58. The town grew around oil and gas exploration during the 1960s, and today a pipeline links it to Edmonton. Vast reservoirs of these resources still lie underneath the ground, but with the recent surge in the price of oil, there is much activity in and around the town. The town has a golf course, two motels, and two restaurants. A campground 24 kilometers (15 miles) southwest of town on the Buffalo River has a few primitive sites, which are free. The other option is **Rainbow Lake Recreation Area,** 48 kilometers (30 miles) south of town, where there's a beach with swimming, fishing, and campsites for $15.

Hay-Zama Lakes

This complex network of lakes, marshes, and streams is one of Canada's largest freshwater wetlands. It covers 800 square kilometers (310 square miles) and is home to more than 200 species of birds, including over 300,000 ducks and geese during fall migration. It's also the main source of the Hay River, which flows north to Great Slave Lake. This fragile ecosystem, 160 kilometers (100 miles) northwest of High Level, is relatively remote and would have remained that way except for the large reservoirs of oil that lie beneath its surface. Oil and birds do not mix, but drilling has gone ahead, with only a small section protected as a wildland provincial park. Strict environmental guidelines mean that most of the mining activity takes place during winter. Although no roads or camping areas are designated around the lakes, many gravel roads used by the natives and oil-exploration personnel lead through the area. The small community of **Zama City,** north of the lakes, has grown around the drilling project.

The Border or Bust

From High Level, it is 191 kilometers (119 miles) to the Alberta–Northwest Territories border. The road follows the Meander River to a town of the same name at the confluence of the Hay River, which then parallels the border. The settlement of **Meander River** is on a Dene Tha Indian Reserve and is noted for its many local artists. Watch for the local rabbit population living beside the road. North of the community, where the highway crosses the Hay River, a gravel road leads 63 kilometers (39 miles) to the oil town of Zama City. Campgrounds are located north of Meander River and just south of the small community of **Steen River,** a base for forest-fire-fighting planes. Alberta's northernmost community is **Indian Cabins,** 14 kilometers (8.7 miles) from the border. The cabins that gave the town its name are gone, but a traditional native cemetery with spirit houses covering the graves is just north of the gas station. In the trees is the scaffold burial site of a child whose body was placed in a hollowed-out log and hung between the limbs of two trees.